MW00761415

BERKSHIRE OUTDOORS

Skiing
Downhill
& Cross Country

Skiing

Downhill & Cross Country

IN THE BERKSHIRE HILLS

TEXT BY LAUREN R. STEVENS
and Lewis C. Cuyler

Illustrations by Alison Kolesar
Maps by Alison Kolesar and Vaughan Gray

BERKSHIRE HOUSE, PUBLISHERS
Great Barrington, Massachusetts

Cover design by Janice Lindstrom. Original design for the text of books in the "Berkshire Outdoors" series by Jane McWhorter. This volume was composed via Pagemaker at Graphic Innovations. Typefaces are Palatino and Helvetica. All skiing maps by Alison Kolesar. Cross country skiing maps are based on U.S. Geological Survey Quadrants. Vaughan Gray drew the supplementary maps. The book was printed by McNaughton & Gunn.

Copyright © 1991 by Berkshire House, Publishers.
All rights reserved. No portion of this book may be repro-
duced — mechanically, electronically, or by any other means,
including photocopying — without the written permission
of the publisher.

Library of Congress Cataloging-in-Publication Data
Stevens, Lauren R., 1938-
Skiing in the Berkshire Hills / by Lauren R. Stevens.
p. cm.
ISBN 0-936399-08-2: $8.95
1. Skis and skiing—Massachusetts—Berkshire Hills—Guide-
books. 2. Cross country skiing—Massachusetts—Berkshire
Hills—Guidebooks.   3. Winter sports—Massachusetts—
Berkshire Hills—Guidebooks. 4. Berkshire Hills (Mass.)—
Description and travel—Guidebooks. I. Title.
GV854.5.M4S74 1990
796.93'09744'1 — dc20   90-81449   CIP

Editors: David Emblidge and Virginia Rowe

Berkshire House, Publishers
Box 915
Great Barrington, MA 01230

Manufactured in the United States of America

First printing February, 1991
10 9 8 7 6 5 4 3 2 1

BERKSHIRE OUTDOORS

. . . is a series of recreation books for the Berkshire County region of western Massachusetts. Berkshire Outdoors titles are designed for both novices and experts, for occasional enthusiasts and every-day exercisers in several sports. Current titles include the book you hold in your hand as well as *Hikes & Walks in the Berkshire Hills* (by Lauren R. Stevens) and *Bike Rides in the Berkshire Hills* (by Lewis C. Cuyler). Each book provides a wide range of carefully researched routes and trails, plus colorful information about the history and cultural attractions in the towns they pass through. The series is dedicated to inspiring respect for the beauty and continued good health of Berkshire's natural environment.

For Becca, Jeff, and Jennie
My companions

BERKSHIRE, THE BERKSHIRES, THE BERKSHIRE HILLS

What is the name of this place, anyway ? The original Berkshire is in England, south of Oxford. There it's pronounced "Bark-sheer." Presumably it was a tanning center, for "berk" derives from "bark," used to make leather. "Shire" means "hilly country county." Certainly trees and hills distinguish Berkshire County in America.

Purists refer to the "Berkshire Hills," meaning specifically what this book calls the southern Taconics, including peaks in New York State. The logic of calling all hills in Berkshire County the Berkshire Hills seems to be gaining acceptance.

"The Berkshires," is a 20th-century term used to publicize the county. This book avoids it, favoring instead just "Berkshire County" or, even more simply, "Berkshire."

TABLE OF CONTENTS

SKIING
Downhill & Cross Country

*[Note: "XC" means "cross country, ski touring or nordic skiing"
and "DH" means "downhill, alpine skiing."]*

SOUTH COUNTY

CENTRAL COUNTY

NORTH COUNTY

OUTSIDE THE COUNTY

APPENDICES

LIST OF MAPS

Maps & Page Numbers	U.S.Geological Survey Quadrangle

SOUTH COUNTY

OUTSIDE THE COUNTY

Woodford, VT

Regional map, inside back cover

United States Geological Survey (USGS) maps are available by quadrangles, as listed above. These do not conform to town boundaries, but are named by the distinguishing feature on each quad. The maps are available at book or sporting goods stores, or from USGS, Reston, VA 22092.

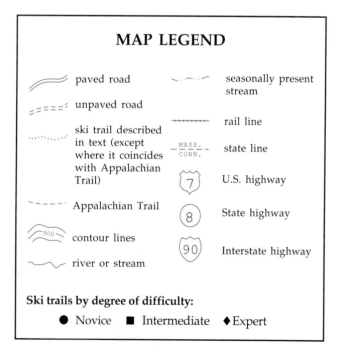

MAP LEGEND

paved road		seasonally present stream
unpaved road		rail line
ski trail described in text (except where it coincides with Appalachian Trail)	MASS. CONN.	state line
	7	U.S. highway
Appalachian Trail	8	State highway
contour lines	90	Interstate highway
river or stream		

Ski trails by degree of difficulty:

● Novice   ■ Intermediate   ◆ Expert

INTRODUCTION

Skiing requires snow, and not much else. Typically Berkshire doesn't get as heavy snowstorms as the New England coast but the snow stays longer. The first flakes fall before Thanksgiving. They disappear. Snow gets more serious in mid-December. It falls in the night; more, a few mornings later. By January it is building up as the temperature drops down. A thaw at the end of January cleans the palate for the February line storms that mark weather fronts. March shows deceptive signs of spring, but the white stuff lingers into April.

Four months, give or take a few weekends. That's for the natural stuff. The snowmakers start spraying air and moisture over the downhill slopes as soon as the nights get cool enough — before Thanksgiving — hoping to build up sufficient depth, together with the snow from the clouds, to last without interruption through the public schools' April vacation week.

If you live here and you take advantage of snow, it goes all too quickly. The opportunities created by snow are worth a visit to Berkshire. Getting out and about, which is so much a part of Berkshire summers, is actually abetted by the cold and slippery surfaces from which some people in some places hide. Skiers can work hard. In fact, the better they are, the harder they know how to work. But skiing contains its own changes of pace, providing profound relaxation and exhilaration. It is a thrill to find what can be seen from high vantage points. Flowing downhill, adjusting to the contours of the land, is also a thrill, as is arriving at that certain rhythm, the stride, of the nordic skier. When you and your environment work together, you can cover more territory more easily than by jogging.

So this book reveals all the local downhill ski spots and the cream of cross country touring locations, both commercial and public. Many other places exist, including your back yard, but *Skiing in the Berkshire Hills* cites the sites local knowledge recommends. This book describes 9 downhill areas and 41 cross country ski spots. It sketches the 23 county towns and cities where most of them take place. Other chapters tell about snow and snowmaking, what plants and animals to look for in winter, what kind of equipment to get and where to find it, and how to get started — which is as much a matter of attitude as anything else. There is information about other indigenous kinds of winter recreation.

In the search for the best snow, the book expands Berkshire a bit to the east and north, to places likely to have good cover even when it's a bit thin down in the valleys. It describes touring centers and woods' tours in nearby Franklin and Hampshire counties in Massachusetts and in extreme southern Vermont. When you can't find snow close at hand, usually you can find it in the highlands on the Berkshire boundaries to the east. When you can't find it in Savoy or Cummington or Worthington, try Woodford, Vermont — in the 100-inch snowbelt. If you can't find it there, it must be summer.

The target is day trips rather than extended outings, ranging from a couple miles to a dozen or so — or a day's outing at a downhill ski area. Nothing is so far away that you would spend more time getting there than actually skiing.

When did alpine skiing in these parts begin? In February 1935 the first ski train from New York chuffed into Pittsfield. To the delight of the locals, 447 skiers disembarked. Each had paid $3 round trip for the privilege of climbing the open slopes of the Clarence J. Bousquet farm at the outskirts of the city.

Bousquet, who had initiated the trip as an experiment, abandoned his other enterprises to cut trails and construct a rope-tow patterned after one that had opened the previous winter in Vermont. He was later to invent a rope-tow gripper, selling more than 200,000 of them before the more comfortable J-bars, T-bars and finally chairs replaced bucking ropes.

Bousquet and Mt. Greylock, where the famous

Thunderbolt racing trail was laid out by the Mt. Greylock Ski Club and cut by the Civilian Conservation Corps, put a focus on Berkshire skiing in the 1930s. In 1938, the Eastern Downhill Championships on the Thunderbolt Ski Trail attracted 6,000 spectators, a huge crowd even by today's standards.

By 1942, it is estimated, the snow trains had brought 40,000 skiers to the Berkshires, most of them skiing at Bousquet and a few at Brodie Mtn. in New Ashford where a second ski operation had opened.

Had it not been for the development of snowmaking in the late 1960s and early 1970s, however, alpine skiing in the Berkshires might have gone the way of the region's textile industry — out. The machine-made snow could guarantee coverage under most weather conditions. During the 1970s and the 1980s, nearly all the areas improved their snowmaking and grooming capacities. Because the size of Berkshire County ski areas enables near-100% coverage, they can seize an advantage over the larger areas to the north in periods of adverse weather.

Most Berkshire downhill ski areas are meticulously tended every night so that they open each morning with fresh powder, or failing that, a cover that has been recycled and aerated in a process that ensures dependable conditions. Several of the better cross country ski touring centers also groom their trails.

The purpose of this book is to pass on information on cross country routes, from Lauren R. Stevens, and downhill routes, from Lewis C. Cuyler, accurate as of winter 1990-91. The text and descriptions should introduce new ideas, reassure you that you are indeed on the right trail, and encourage you — because the most important message from research refers not to the details of geography. Rather it is that even when the weather is a bit uncertain, the distance seems a little far, you've got other things to do, or you're not feeling quite 100%, going out will always make you feel good.

Feel good because skiing is good exercise — the best,

some experts say. This book should help you determine which distances and degrees of difficulty are healthiest for you. Good because the scenery varies from serene to breathtaking, and there is no better way to see it than to get yourself there under your own power, true personal empowerment. Good because you are enjoying rather than enduring the cold and snow. Good because you and I need to rediscover ourselves periodically in the Berkshire outdoors — when the elements test us.

Thanks

My thanks to Lew Cuyler, who not only wrote the downhill and equipment portions of this book, but shared his knowledge of cross country skiing as well. Thanks also to Pamela Weatherbee for taking me for a walk in the snow — which became "What to See in Winter" (first published in *Berkshires Week*). Robert Goodell and John Eusden introduced me to cross country skiing some 25 years ago. Many other friends throughout the county greatly broadened my knowledge of skiable spots. John Blackmer, James Caffrey,David Emblidge, Allen Hart, Robert Hatton, Conrad Oman, David Robb, Robert Spencer, and Whit Griswold's *Berkshire Trails for Walking and Ski Touring* (now out of print), introduced me to specific trails.

HOW TO USE THIS BOOK

This book tries its best to be accurate and helpful. Neither the author nor the publisher can be responsible beyond that effort. Many things, both natural and manmade, are subject to change and out of the author's control. And, with the best intentions, errors are possible.

Key Terms, Important Names, Abbreviations

Some definitions are in order. Once all skiers used the same equipment. Downhill or alpine skiing, nowadays, refers to high boots, short and wide skis, lifts to get you to the top of the hill, and groomed snow. Cross country or nordic skiing ("xc") employs low boots, generally attached only at the toe; and light, narrow skis either waxed or otherwise designed so that you can ski uphill as well as downhill. John Caldwell has defined cross country skiing as analogous to walking in bedrooms slippers, which you slide along the floor. Cross country skiing (xc) is further subdivided into those primarily interested in racing and those out for a tour. Either group may choose to move by the traditional diagonal stride, with skis parallel, or the newer skating stride, pushing off skis at an angle. Skating has been the rage over several years, because it is faster, but the grace of diagonal striding seems to be returning. Skating works best on groomed surfaces, whereas diagonal striding works best where a track has been set but can also take you into unprepared areas.

The word "facilities," as used here, refers to manmade structures that could convenience the skier, specifically toilets, which can be flush-type or outhouses. The initials "HQ" refer to headquarters for either state-owned or privately owned properties open to the public. "CCC" stands for Civilian Conservation Corps, the 1930s project for putting men to work, often in state forests, that resulted in many improvements in roads, trails, forestry and buildings.

"AMC" refers to the Appalachian Mtn. Club, the hiking and environmentally oriented not-for-profit organization. It is related to but not the same as the Appalachian Trail Conference, the group of local organizations that maintain the "AT," the foot trail from Georgia to Maine. Another not-for-profit environmental organization, the Massachusetts Audubon Society, a separate entity from the National Audubon Society, owns and maintains two sanctuaries in Berkshire, both of which are described in the text. Another major land owner is also private, the Trustees of Reservations ("TTOR"), a statewide group originally founded as analogous to a public library: a resource available to the public for beautiful and historic places. Four skis here take place on TTOR property.

Another private group, the New England Forestry Foundation, owns and maintains the Dorothy Frances Rice Sanctuary. Ski tours also cross lands of Simon's Rock of Bard College, Buxton School, the Sterling and Francine Clark Art Institute, Williams College, and other private landowners, who should be shown all courtesy.

A quarter of the land in Berkshire is protected in some way, mostly the 95,000 acres of the state's forests and parks. The Division of Fisheries and Wildlife, municipal watersheds, the Berkshire Natural Resources Council and local land trusts, and the private groups mentioned above also protect land while making it available to the public. This structure of intelligent and sensitive public land ownership is the reason, less obvious than topography, why Berkshire County is skiers' heaven.

Berkshire skiers are also indebted to numerous groups that lay out, blaze and maintain trails, such as: the Appalachian Trail Conference members, the Massachusetts' Division of Forests and Parks, the Vermont Agency for Natural Resources, the Green Mtn. Club, the Taconic Hiking Club of New York, and the Williams (College) Outing Club.

Trail Indicators

Most of the trails in this book are marked by blazes: a daub of paint, at eye level usually, directly on a tree or on wood or metal attached to a tree or driven into the ground. A common route for two trails may be blazed with two colors.

Two blazes, one above the other, signals a sharp turn or other unusual circumstance ahead. In this county, the north-south long trails such as the Appalachian Trail (AT) and Taconic Crest Trail (TCT) are blazed with rectangular white daubs (which can be hard to pick up in winter); side trails are blazed blue; and trails that don't connect are blazed orange — with local exceptions.

Berkshire Area Code

The area code for all of Berkshire County and the Massachusetts counties on its eastern flank (Franklin, Hampshire, Hampden) is 413; we cite local exchanges only in our listing of the telephone numbers of the various Berkshire ski areas. For the few Vermont areas listed, the area code is 802.

Additional Maps

To find some of the not-so-obvious corners of the county, a supplement to regular road maps is advisable. One is Jimapco Map C12, Berkshire County, MA, 3rd edition, $2.95. It is available in bookstores, drugstores, and newspaper stores or from Jimapco, Box 1137, Clifton Park, NY 12065; 1-800-MAPS 123. A lovely road map is also available at the County Surveyors' Office, Bowes Building, Park Sq., Pittsfield, MA 01201. The List of Maps in the front of this book indicates the U.S. Geological Survey quadrangle(s) for each ski. These maps are available at bookstores and sporting goods stores. They provide the base for virtually all county maps.

Organization

The book breaks the county into three parts, so that you can refer easily to those places nearest you: South, Central, and North, with the additional category of Outside the County. Here's a thought: try places in the other locations as well as closest to home. The differences are significant, and contrast helps to define what is special about each.

NORTH COUNTY
Adams (Population: 9,706)
Cheshire (3,492)
Clarksburg (1,866)
Florida (735)
New Ashford (193)
North Adams (16,271)
Savoy (595)
Williamstown (8,361)

CENTRAL COUNTY
Becket (1,524)
Dalton (7, 212)
Hancock (800)
Hinsdale (2,011)
Lanesborough (3,100)
Lenox (5,557)
Peru (724)
Pittsfield (49,418)
Richmond (1,701)
Washington (602)
Windsor (638)

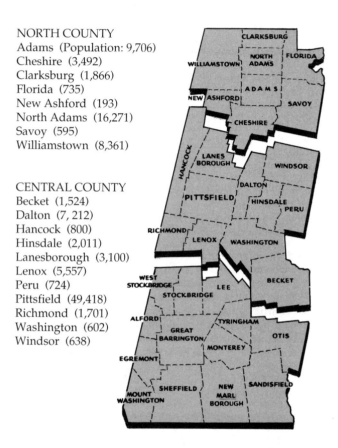

SOUTH COUNTY
Alford (367)
Egremont (1,052)
Great Barrington (7,014)
Lee (6,020)
Monterey (841)
Mount Washington (120)

New Marlborough (1,098)
Otis (963)
Sandisfield (735)
Sheffield (3,264)
Stockbridge (2,581)
Tyringham (365)
West Stockbridge (1,425)

TRANSPORTATION

Getting to the Berkshires

BY CAR

From Manhattan: Take the Major Deegan Expressway or the Henry Hudson Parkway to the Saw Mill River Parkway, then proceed north on the Taconic State Parkway. For the southern Berkshires, exit the Taconic at Hillsdale, Claverack, Rte. 23 and follow 23 east, towards Hillsdale and on to Gt. Barrington. For Stockbridge, Lee, and Lenox, (and all points in South and Central county) proceed up Rte. 7. For Williamstown and all of northern Berkshire, you might want to proceed farther up the Taconic and exit at Rte. 295, leading to Stephentown, then follow Rte. 43 through Hancock to Williamstown.

From New Jersey, Pennsylvania and the South: Rte. 22 north is a good choice for local color, and you can pick it up as far south as Armonk or Bedford in Westchester County, New York. From Rte. 22, farther upstate, turn right at Hillsdale on 23 east toward Gt. Barrington. For the most direct route from New Jersey, Pennsylvania and the South, take the New York Thruway to I-84 east; at the Taconic parkway go north to Rte. 23 for southern Berkshire or Rte. 295 for northern Berkshire.

From Connecticut and/or New York Metro Area: Rte. 7 is a scenic route, which can be picked up at Danbury, via I-684 and I-84. To arrive in southeastern Berkshire, Rte. 8 is a quick and scenic drive as it follows the Farmington River north.

From Boston and the East: The Massachusetts Turnpike is the quickest, easiest and one of the more scenic routes west to southern Berkshire. West of the Connecticut River, you can get off the turnpike at Exit 3 and take Rte. 202 south to Rte. 20 west and pick up Rte. 23 west at Woronoco for the best route to Otis Ridge, Butternut Basin and Catamount ski areas. Most people stay on the turnpike right into Berkshire County, exiting either at Lee or West Stockbridge.

(Continued on pg. 28)

BERKSHIRE ACCESS

Using Tanglewood (on the Stockbridge — Lenox line) as the Berkshire reference point, the following cities are this close.

CITY	TIME	MILES
Albany	1 hr	50
Boston	2½ hrs	135
Bridgeport	2 hrs	110
Danbury	1¾ hrs	85
Hartford	1½ hrs	70
Montreal	5 hrs	275
New Haven	2½ hrs	115
New York City	3 hrs	150
Philadelphia	4½ hrs	230
Providence	2½ hrs	125
Springfield	¾ hr	35
Waterbury	1½ hrs	75
Washington, DC	7 hrs	350
Worcester	1¾ hrs	90

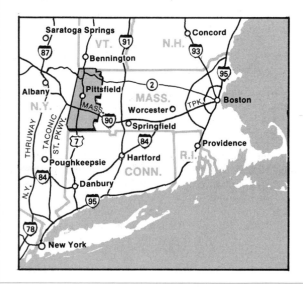

Berkshire County is 56 miles south to north, from Sheffield to Williamstown. Depending on the season and the weather, it's normally a two-hour leisurely drive up Rte. 7. Because of the mountain ranges that run along this route, east-west travel across the county remains much more difficult, with all the county's east-west routes (2 in the north; 9, midcounty; and 23 in the south) being tricky drives in freezing or snowy weather.

(Continued from pg. 25)

If you're coming west to the Berkshires from more northern latitudes, eastern entry to Berkshire County can be gained by driving the original Mohawk Trail, an Indian byway. Also known as Rte. 2, this is the most direct way to Jiminy Peak and Brodie Mountain skiing .

From Hartford: The quickest route by far is I-91 north to the Massachusetts Turnpike west. Then proceed as in directions for Massachusetts Turnpike travel from Boston.

From Montreal or Albany: Leaving Canada, take I-87 (known as "the Northway") south to Albany, and exit at Rte. 7 to Rte. 2 toward Williamstown, or continue on I-87 south to I-90 east, connecting then to the Massachusetts Turnpike which is the continuation of I-90 east. Exit at either Canaan, New York, or Lee, Massachusetts.

BY BUS

From Manhattan   (3.5 hours): Bonanza (212-564-8484) serves the Berkshires out of New York City's Port Authority Bus Terminal at 40th St. between 8th and 9th Aves. Tickets may be purchased at the Greyhound ticket windows (212-971-6363) near 8th Ave. Boarding is down the escalators at the center of the terminal, and then to the right, usually at Gate 13. Bonanza runs three buses daily: 8:45 a.m., 1:45 p.m., and 4:45 p.m. On Friday afternoons, there's an express to the Berkshires, leaving Port Authority around 4:45 and arriving in Gt. Barrington about 7:50. There is also an additional Friday bus, leaving Port Authority at 6:45. The 1991 round-trip ticket price is $44 to Gt. Barrington, with a same-day round trip priced at $33. Berkshire locales marked with an asterisk are Flag Stops, where you must wave to the bus driver in order to be picked up.

Berkshire Phone Numbers for New York Buses

Canaan, CT	Canaan Pharmacy, Main St.	203-824-5481
Gt. Barrington	Bill's Pharmacy, 362 Main St.	528-1590

Hillsdale, NY	*Junction Rtes. 22 & 23 800-556-3815
Lee	McClelland Drugs, 43 Main St. 243-0135
Lenox	New Dimensions, Walker St. 637-2588
New Ashford	*Entrance to Brodie Mt. Ski Area, Rte. 7 800-556-3815
No. Adams	Bus Terminal (Englander Coach Lines); Oasis Plaza,
	148 American Legion Dr. 662-2016
Pittsfield	Bus Terminal, 57 South Church St. 442-4451
Sheffield	*First Agricultural Bank, Rte. 7 800-556-3815
So. Egremont	*Gaslight Store 800-556-3815
Stockbridge	Chamber of Commerce Booth, Main St. 298-3344
Williamstown	Williams Inn, Main St. 458-2665

From Boston (3.5 hrs.): Bonanza, Englander and Greyhound serve the Berkshires from Boston out of the Greyhound Terminal at 10 St. James Ave. (617-423-5810). Bonanza/Greyhound serves Lee, Lenox and Pittsfield; Englander serves Williamstown and No. Adams. Greyhound/Trailways runs two buses daily to Pittsfield out of the Trailways Terminal at 555 Atlantic Ave. Trailways' 1991 weekday round-trip ticket price to Pittsfield was $26, weekend round-trip ticket, $30.

Berkshire Phone Numbers for Boston Buses:

Lee	McClelland Drugs, 43 Main St. 243-0135
Lenox	Hagyard Pharmacy (Greyhound Agency)
	4 Housatonic St. 637-0048
No. Adams	Englander Coach Lines, Oasis Plaza, ... 664-4588 or
	148 American Legion Dr. 662-2016
Pittsfield	Bus Terminal, 57 South Church St. 442-4451
Williamstown	Williams Inn, 1090 Main St. 458-2665

From Hartford (1.75 hrs.): The Arrow Line runs one bus daily, with a second on Friday and Sunday into Pittsfield from the Greyhound Terminal at 409 Church St., Hartford (203-547-1500). Arrow's 1991 round-trip ticket price was $38.

From Montreal (6 hrs.): Greyhound runs south to the Albany Greyhound Terminal. Connect to Pittsfield as noted below.

From Albany (1 hr.): The Arrow Line runs two buses from Albany to Pittsfield on Friday and Sunday only; 1991 round-trip ticket price was $15. Bonanza runs two buses daily from Albany to Pittsfield. Greyhound runs one bus daily with an additional one on Friday and Sunday; 1991 round-trip ticket was $15 on Bonanza and $11 on Greyhound.

BY TRAIN

From Manhattan: Amtrak (800-872-7245) can help you get to the Berkshires, but not all the way. Their turboliner from Grand Central Station runs frequently along the Hudson River. For southern Berkshire, stay aboard till Hudson; for northern Berkshire, carry on to Rensselaer. Limousine or taxi service can be arranged for the 40-mi. trip from Hudson to southern Berkshire or from Rensselaer to northern Berkshire (46 mi.).

From Hudson .... Star City Taxi 518-828-3355
From Rensselaer .... AAA Limousine 518-456-5030
                                        Diamond Limousine 518-283-8000,
                                                             800-448-0844

From Boston: Amtrak runs a single train daily through the Berkshires, starting from Boston's South Station. The Pittsfield depot has no actual station; it's just a shelter. (To find the depot: take West St. westwards past the Hilton; at the first light, turn right onto Center St.; take the next right onto Depot St.; the shelter is on the left.) Anyone boarding the train in Pittsfield must purchase tickets on the train; the 1991 round-trip ticket price ranged from $25 each way to $38 round trip, depending on time of travel and seat availability. Private compartments are also available, ranging from $46.50 supplementary for a single compartment to $79 supplementary for a double compartment.

From Montreal: Amtrak runs one train daily from Montreal through Albany. The 1991 round-trip ticket price was $60, excluding holiday periods. During the Thanksgiving, Christmas and New Year's seasons, the round-trip rate rises to $92. There is no same-day train connection from this run to the Berkshires; to get here by hired car, see information above on limousine or bus service from Albany.

From Albany: Amtrak has a single Pittsfield-bound train daily from the Albany/Rensselaer Depot on East St. (2 mi. from downtown Albany). The 1991 ticket fare was $10 one way, and ranges from $15 to $17 round trip depending on time of travel and seat availability.

BY PLANE

If you own a small airplane or decide to charter one, you can fly directly to the Berkshires, landing at Gt. Barrington, Pittsfield or No. Adams airports.

From New York City: There are several charter air companies in the metropolitan New York Area that will fly you from La Guardia, JFK or other airports near New York to any of the Berkshire airports. Their 1991 estimated rates ran from $675 to $1000 one way, for a twin-engine airplane (holds five plus the pilot). Airlines currently flying these routes include:

    Aircraft Charter Group 800-553-3590
    Chester Air, Chester, CT.........800-752-6371
    Long Island Airways 800-645-9572

and from Westchester County:

    Panorama (White Plains airport) 914-328-9800
          or,if calling from New York, 718-507-9800
    Richmor Aviation 800-331-6101

From Boston: Estimated rates for 1991 ran $275 to $600 for a twin-engine airplane (holds five plus the pilot).

    Aerotransit 508-777-3250
    Bird Airfleet 508-372-6566
    Wiggins Airways ....617-762-5690, Ext. 251

From Hartford: Bradley Airport in Hartford handles numerous domestic and international airlines, so you can fly to Bradley from nearly anywhere. From there, charter air service to the Berkshires is available through any of the companies listed under "From Boston" or through the Berkshire County companies listed below.

From Albany: Albany is terminus for a substantial volume of domestic jet traffic and, being under an hour from the Berkshires by car, is the closest you can get to these hills by jet. Charter connector flights from Albany to the Berkshires are available through Page Flight (518-869-0253) or through the Berkshire County companies listed below.

In Berkshire County: Three aviation companies in Berkshire County operate air taxi service to just about any other northeastern airport.

Berkshire Aviation .... Gt. Barrington Airport
                                              528-1010, 528-1061
Lyon Aviation .... Pittsfield Airport
                                              443-6700
Esposito Flying Service ... Harriman & West Airport,
                                              No. Adams 663-3330

These local carriers' 1991 rates for a twin-engine plane (holds five plus the pilot) averaged $200 to Albany, $550 to Boston, $235 to Hartford, $700 to La Guardia or JFK, and $495 to Teterboro, New Jersey (at the foot of the George Washington Bridge). They also have single-engine planes (holds three plus pilot) for roughly 35-40% less, but these are dependent on weather conditions.

LODGING AND DINING

Berkshire offers a host of possibilities for lodging and dining, from the humble to the luxurious. The popularity of the area as a tourist destination means that those who want to visit in busy seasons must plan ahead. Lodging reservations are particularly important. We recommend two approaches to finding a place to stay and deciding where to eat. *The Berkshire Book: A Complete Guide*, by Jonathan Sternfield, from the publishers of this skiing guide, is a thoroughly researched travel book, covering not only lodging and dining, but culture, recreation, shopping and many other topics as well. *The New York Times* said its recommendations were "right on the money." It is available from bookstores throughout the United States or from the publisher (Berkshire House, Box 915, Gt. Barrington, MA 01230; $14.95). Or you can call the Berkshire Visitors Bureau (413-443-9186) to ask for their package of brochures about lodging and dining possibilities. Both *The Berkshire Book* and the Visitors Bureau provide telephone numbers for Chamber of Commerce and other lodging reservations services.

Jonathan Sternfield's *The Berkshire Book* actually reviews restaurants and food purveyors, and you might enjoy seeing whether your opinions harmonize with his.

Camping in State Parks and Forests

The situation with state parks and forests as of this writing is somewhat clouded. Given the current budgetary crisis in Massachusetts there is a strong possibility that a number of state parks and forests will be closed or higher fees may be required. An advance call to ascertain the status of these areas before planning a trip is highly recommended.

BERKSHIRE SKI REPORTS AND WEATHER INFORMATION

Ski Reports

Recorded messages about downhill ski conditions in the Berkshires are available at these telephone numbers:
Berkshire Ski Phone 413-499-7669
Eastern Ski Reports from Area Codes 212-, 516-, 718-, and 914-, dial 394-3333.

Ski condition reports are broadcast twice daily by radio stations in these Berkshire towns (times are subject to change):

South County — Gt. Barrington
WSBS-AM 860 at 8:15 a.m. and 12:15 p.m.
WBBS-FM 105, 7:45 and 11:45 a.m.

Central County — Pittsfield
WBEC-AM 1420 at 6:05 p.m.
WBEC-FM 105.5 at 4:25 p.m.

North County — No. Adams
WMNB-AM 1230 at 7:30 a.m. and 5:30 p.m.
WMNB-FM 100.1, 8:00 a.m. and 6:00 p.m.

Information about conditions at cross country skiing centers is best obtained by calling the centers themselves. Trail descriptions in this book include telephone numbers, if available.

Weather Information

Berkshire weather reports are available by telephone from several numbers. Here are three (area code 413): South County, 243-0065; Central County, 499-2627; North County, 743-3313.

Weather varies with elevation as well as south to north. Furthermore, the Berkshire area is cooler than areas to the south and east because it is affected by the prevailing westerly wind rather than the proximity of the ocean.

Average Temperature

December	25.0
January	21.2
February	23.5
March	33.4

Average Precipitation

Snow	70 "
Rain	36.14 "
Total	43.14 "

SAFETY

Winter has a way of focusing your attention. You don't have to worry about nuisances, like poison ivy or stinging wasps or slithering snakes. You prepare for cold and judge snow conditions, trying to avoid high wind and heavy snowfall that could make it difficult to get where you want to go. These are not trivial concerns, even when you are only a short distance from the base lodge or some other form of civilization.

While serious and demanding attention, the dangers of skiing are manageable with good sense. The rewards, including promotion of good health, far outweigh the risks. Just getting out and moving about at a time of the year when people are apt to feel closed in is beneficial. The exercise — stirring up the muscles, blood, and breakfast — is good for the body. And good for the mind.

A Few Basic Rules

Here are a few succinct rules, all of which are summed up in the first.

1. Take a few minutes before you go out to think through what you're going to do.
2. Wear layered clothing, so that you can layer up or down, as the circumstance warrants.
3. Carry cold weather cream to cover bare skin on your face. Wear a hat you can pull down over your ears and mittens to stay warm.
4. Drink plenty of water.
5. Never assume that the ice over the pond is thick enough to hold you until you test it.
6. For ski tourers: signs and blazes are constructions of man and cannot always be trusted. Leave the cares of civilization behind but take along a map (such as the ones in this book) a compass, and a watch.

Staying Warm

Your body lets off heat through your fingers, which are like the ribs of a hot water radiator. Gloves isolate your fingers, so that they don't benefit from each other's warmth; hence your hands feel colder. Wear mittens. Most heat from the body leaves from your head, so that is the most important part of the body — and also the easiest — to keep covered. Wear a cap. Although synthetic fabrics perform well, in general, loose clothing which traps air, keeps you warmer than slick tights. Wool socks have the unique features of cushioning your feet from your boots and wicking off moisture, as well as trapping air. And when the wind is up, keep off frostbite by smearing your forehead and cheeks with a cream or vasoline. Eat warm food, when possible. Hot soup from a thermos is a wonderful treat on the trail. Cook out on the grills at state parks. Take fruit and sweets, for energy.

Taking alcohol or doing drugs in winter weather could dull your awareness of your body's warning signs of cold, leading to disorientation or disaster.

First Aid

Frostbite is the most obvious concern, and it is best treated in the wilderness by warming the affected part gradually by applying snow. Cold and snow are actually beneficial in reducing bleeding. Vasoline applied to exposed surfaces prevents frostbite or windburn. Don't forget sunglasses on those brilliant days when the snow increases the intensity of the sun.

Hypothermia, or a significant lowering of the body temperature, does not require extremely low temperatures. For example, getting wet and just cool can produce this condition. Clothing is most important (see above). After you've raised a sweat, say skiing up a hill, you may need an additional layer to keep you warm in the wind of the summit. Someone suffering from this condition is likely to become disoriented, often further exacerbating the situation.

Pay attention to your signs. If, in spite of your exercise, you are not warming up or if you are beginning to feel panicky, head for shelter. If you come across someone else in this condition, do everything you possibly can to warm that person up.

If you are injured at a downhill area, wait as comfortably as you can for the ski patrol. No heroics. Don't try to hobble down the hill with a broken limb or gashed head.

At commercial cross country areas or even managed noncommercial areas, someone will "sweep," that is, ski over, all the trails at the end of the day. You may not want to wait that long for assistance. It's not a bad idea to carry a whistle. A small first-aid kit in a fanny pack can certainly help.

If you are touring in the woods, you should not be alone. If you find yourself injured with no help immediately available, your best bet is to give yourself a few minutes to think through the situation before you do anything.

FOR THE HEALTH OF IT

At nearly any age and level of ability, you can ski. The problem of learning how to ski derives from our attitude of having to do something well. Relax. Ski to enjoy. Go only as fast as you want to. Tackle only as difficult a slope as you want. Don't worry what you look like. Laugh a lot.

Equipment and care of slopes have improved to the point that the downhill skier is far less likely to break something than was true in the past. Cross country is even less dangerous, although of course it is always possible to wrench a knee, dislocate a shoulder, or tear thumb ligaments. Avoid icy patches. Skiers can suffer if they are not in reasonably good shape — although nordic skiing is a fine route to shape. One reason for the relative safety of cross country skiing is that the low boots are only attached to the ski at the toe, so that twisting doesn't need to occur in your leg. Sophisticated xc skiers who attach the heel in order to negotiate steeper downhills incur greater risk.

Cross country skiing is a total body exercise. Your legs do most of the work but about one-fourth of your forward motion comes from your arms through your poles, if you are doing it correctly. It tones up legs, arms, shoulders, back, chest and buttocks. According to health columnist Jane Brody, "It can also be a high-intensity aerobic activity that can significantly improve cardiovascular function and enhance the body's ability to use oxygen efficiently" (phew) — assuming you work at least 15 or 20 minutes at a time. Done steadily, xc ski uses 600 to 900 calories an hour, an amount matched only by handball among conditioning activities.

It can be done in a much more leisurely manner, too, as a way of walking in the woods in winter.

Getting Started

Some people believe intensely in self-improvement and feel an activity is incomplete unless they have LEARNED HOW TO DO IT. That's fine. These folks will be most satisfied if they approach skiing, whether downhill or cross country, by taking lessons. These are available at all the downhill and ski touring resorts, and through various sporting goods stores.

Other people regard recreation not as a skill to be mastered so much as a means towards enjoyment. These folks can imagine trying out skiing without enlisting in basic training. Some lessons along the way are appropriate, but they can find out if they enjoy the feeling first.

These people will borrow or rent equipment. They won't start at a resort, necessarily, but maybe in the back yard or on the nearby golf course. (Some courses are delighted to have skiers, some aren't.) They won't worry about lifts, right away, realizing that they will learn a lot about how skis work by trying to get up the slope; they will also get some good exercise that way. Making their own way uphill will tighten muscles and prevent injuries.

If all this sounds familiar, that's because it describes the way people used to learn how to ski, before all experiences were packaged and sold. No special clothes, other than boots, required; no travel, if you are fortunate enough to be in Berkshire County; not much of an investment. Of course, if going to Aspen is the goal and skiing the excuse, it won't work.

Don't buy the line that somehow you're going to ruin the possibility of ever learning how to do it right if you get out and struggle on your own a bit. Don't buy the line that you're more likely to hurt yourself. Few beginners in their back yards have to put up with hotdogs careening by them at 50 m.p.h.

Ski touring is best seen as the nicest way to get where you want to go in winter conditions. People who like to be outside, like to be outside in the winter, too, only you have to deal with that white stuff. Rather than letting it be an obstacle, use it.

This isn't the place to describe how to ski. As far as touring is concerned, it's basically sliding one foot ahead of the other, a lot like walking. If stopping becomes important and no other means is handy, fall. To turn, take your weight off the outside ski, point it in the direction you want to go, take your weight off the other ski and adjust its direction.

When you are starting to feel comfortable, don't just go out to ski. Ski to get some place you want to go; maybe because you've never been there, maybe because you've never been there in winter. Go. Carry a few amenities in a pack, all the way from a trail mix of raisins, nuts and other goodies to a complete picnic. Who says you can't eat out in the winter? Some sandwiches taste better frozen.

A number of the state ski spots described here include picnic grounds with grills. Take some charcoal and lighter fluid in the car. Have a cookout while you ski. Warm your hands and feet as you grill your steak or tofuburger. Toast marshmallows. Go winter camping in shelters or cabins such as are described here. It's fun to get water by cutting a hole in the ice of your favorite lake. Try fishing it; you might catch supper.

Ski to a restaurant or an inn. Not only trails but many old roads, unplowed in the winter, are ideal for cross country travel. In the middle of the woods in the Yaw Pond ski, you come across a sign directing you to a local inn. Ski to friends' houses. If you happen to have vacant land nearby, develop a trail of your own, maybe to some special spot where you like to meditate. After a good storm, you can go to the post office on skis — they do it all the time in Norway.

The point is that if you find yourself in a place where there's winter, you're either going to be grouchy from December through February or you're going to get a kick out of it.

Most of your skiing will be during daylight hours, which are somewhat restricted in midwinter. Be sure to pick a night of full moon for a ski. You will discover that the snow reflects light, so that it is much easier to see where you're going than you might expect. You will discover that the wind generally dies down at night, so that even as the temperature falls you don't feel as cold as during the day. Skiing in moonlight is like floating between two surfaces: you know the sky is up there somewhere and somewhere below is solid ground. But you and your skis just swish along, disconnected.

It is harder to judge depth, so that slopes surprise you. But the real danger is only that you will want to ski all night, caught in a natural and healthy high.

After you've found it fun, you may want to develop special skills, more towards downhill or more towards xc racing. Maybe you want to learn how to climb mountains with skins on the bottom of your skis or maybe you want to try telemark turns, those deep knee bends you occasionally see someone using to ski a downhill slope with xc skis.

Time enough to get serious about it after you've learned you like it.

BERKSHIRE HISTORY

Both natural history and social history in Berkshire are tales of ups and downs. Looking at both from the end of the 20th century, you may feel some past time was better than the present, but it ain't necessarily so. The county testifies that geography, for all our veneer of civilization, is still destiny. And this county, now, maintains a delicate balance of being close to but not too close to the Boston-Washington megalopolis that holds down the East Coast. It is an accessible hinterland. It has the position and the resources to rise up into the future.

Six hundred million years ago the area was down, under the ocean, which was at work forming the rocks. It was warm and wet, with sandy beaches and clear, shallow waters. The lapping waves built up beaches that turned to sandstone, which in turn metamorphosed into quartzite — the erosion-resistant backbone of many of the county's ridges. Shelled marine animals built coral reefs, which calcified into limestone. The deposits of this alkaline agent, mined on the side of Mt. Greylock in Adams, protect the area from the worst ravages of acid precipitation today. Some of that limestone was recrystalized into marble, snowy chunks of which grace the hiking trails and can be inspected at the Natural Bridge in Clarksburg. Muddy offshore sediments settled to form shales and then schists, crystalline rocks that fracture cleanly. The bands of granite that run through the southern part of the county antedate the metamorphic rock.

The continents began to shift, in response to subterranean pressure. At a speed of about an inch a year over 150 million years, the land masses that would one day be North America, Africa, and Europe moved towards each other, closing the proto-Atlantic ocean. Several arcs of offshore volcanic islands were shoved onto the continent by a series of slow but cataclysmic collisions known as the Taconic Orogeny (Taconic mountain building). The entire continental shelf was squeezed into a series of folds, the monumental forerunners of the Appalachian Range. The bases of these mountains, some Himalayan in height, must have just about filled Berkshire, when the county reached for the sky. Then the continents began to pull apart, as they are still doing.

As soon as mountains were stacked up, the process of erosion began. Rain fell, forming rivers that still drain these hills, but in those days more vigorously carving a landscape unrooted by vegetation. Not only water but wind sculpted Berkshire hills, raging unbroken by trees and shrubs. The rugged landscape was tamed, waiting only for plants to soften it.

Less than two million years ago the first of a succession of four ice sheets ground down in response to a cooling climate. These mile-high glaciers brought debris, gravel and rocks, which they deposited around the nubbins of mountains that remained. Glacial lakes covered most of North County and a good portion of the south. Because the Hoosac Valley was preglacial, once the melt set in, the Hoosic River returned to flowing across the north-south path of the ice. This and the Upper Ammonoosuc in New Hampshire are the only rivers in New England to flow from southwest to northeast. Nor were the beds of the Housatonic or Westfield much altered. The Farmington River ran up against a load of glacial trash that turned its general southerly course in Connecticut.

The ice withdrew as recently as 10,000 years ago. Vegetation and then wildlife followed its retreating edge. Perhaps a few of the earliest North American inhabitants, having boated or walked across the land bridge from Asia, were in Berkshire to bid farewell to the ice. Gradually, the evergreen forest moved north, lingering only on the tops of   the highest ridges, while the broad-leaved, deciduous forest moved in, characterized in North County by sugar maple and in the south by oak, with their associated pines, ash, beech, birch and alder.

The rocky steepness of the county does not lend itself to leisurely flowing water and big lakes. With the exception of the southern reach of the Housatonic, which meanders in curlicues through Sheffield, Berkshire rivers retain little water and rush to their destinations. What lakes the county has, it owes to the efforts of 19th-century industrialists to

create a head or a reservoir to provide a year-round flow
of water for power or other manufacturing processes: Otis
Reservoir, Cheshire Reservoir, Pontoosuc, Onota, and others.

Seen from above, the county presents the ridges that
remain from the north-south running folds, the Taconics
along the New York line, the lower end of the Green Mountains
protruding over the Vermont line, the Hoosacs filling the
northeast quadrant, the Southern Berkshire Plateau filling the
southeast quadrant, and a line of river valleys, just to the left
of center, made up of the Hoosic and Housatonic — albeit
flowing in opposite directions — that meet in New Ashford.

The Greylock massif stands as a peninsula to the Taconics
—as indeed it was when glacial Lake Bascom filled the Hoosac
Valley up to the 1,300-ft. contour. Therefore it may be
appropriate that the summit of Greylock lifts a War Memorial
Tower, designed originally to be a lighthouse for the Charles
River estuary, bearing a beacon that can be seen by people
navigating most of the county. If any man-made feature is
needed to unite a geographical area so well defined
topographically, it would be that tower and the roads it guards
(Rtes. 2, 7 and 8).

Getting in and out and around Berkshire used to be a
problem. The native Americans generally thought of the area
as removed from their Hudson River homes, a hunting ground
to visit in the summer. The Mahicans entered from the south
or north, along the river valleys. Although the Bay Colony
claimed the land early on, Bay Colony residents found it tough
to surmount the Berkshire barrier to the east. Early settlers
found it easier to enter along the valleys, a few Dutch infiltrating
through the Taconics from New York, but especially residents
from the area now known as Connecticut, up the Housatonic.
Thus the county was settled from the south to the north, the
earliest towns in the south dating to the first quarter of the 18th
century. The main roads, railroads and even sewer lines now
follow the valleys.

The European settlers were primarily farmers, typically
working the bottom lands and, as they filled up, moving up
the sides of the hills. Remains of walls, cellar holes, and
orchards such as you come across in your ambles remind you

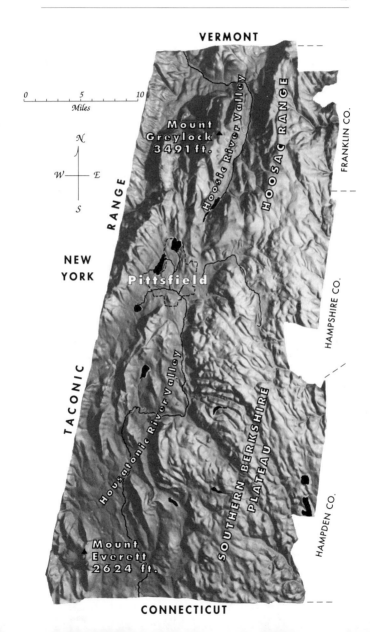

VERMONT

0 5 10
Miles

N
W E
S

RANGE

Mount
Greylock
3491 ft.

Hoosic River Valley

HOOSAC RANGE

FRANKLIN CO.

NEW
YORK

Pittsfield

HAMPSHIRE CO.

TACONIC

Housatonic River Valley

SOUTHERN BERKSHIRE PLATEAU

HAMPDEN CO.

Mount
Everett
2624 ft.

CONNECTICUT

that even what seem now lofty ridges were at one time home, especially for those who made their living grazing cattle or merino sheep. In Stockbridge, the English Society for the Propagation of the Gospel in Foreign Parts set up an Indian mission, which gradually acceded to the land hunger of the Europeans. By the time of the Revolution, virtually all native Americans had departed.

As a farmer installed a mill to grind his corn or saw his wood, and his neighbors came to have him do their milling, so industry followed the plough. What began as groupings to protect against French or Indian raids became trading centers. Specialty manufactures, depending on natural resources, developed, such as glass, paper, charcoal, and textiles. Even education can be seen as an industry depending on natural resources. After all, Thoreau said of Williams College's position at the foot of Greylock: "It would be no small advantage if every college were thus located at the base of a mountain, as good at least as one well-endowed professorship . . . . Some will remember, no doubt, not only that they went to college, but that they went to the mountain." In Berkshire County, three of the four colleges and many of the secondary schools are at the base of mountains.

The opening of the Erie Canal in 1825, providing a practical means for younger residents to head west where the thick topsoil had a lot fewer glacial stones than that of Berkshire, drained the county of human resources. One by one lights winked out on the sidehill farms. Whereas by the middle of the century three-quarters of the trees had been stripped for pasture land or to feed the insatiable maws of the railroad, the county has been revegetating for 150 years. In Berkshire that ratio is inverted today. The county is three-quarters wooded, which is why coyotes, bear, beaver, turkeys, and even moose are returning to join the populous deer and smaller animals.

The most important industrial event in the county's history happened in 1886, when William Stanley linked 25 shops along the main street of Great Barrington in the world's first commercial electric system. That, in turn, drew the General Electric Co. to Stanley's shop in Pittsfield. GE has been here ever since, the largest employer in the county. The second most important industrial event was the opening of the Hoosac Tunnel, at 4.75 miles the longest bore in the world in 1875, breaking through the Berkshire barrier for direct train service in the North County from Boston to Albany.

Yet even in the heady days when industry was king — the population of Pittsfield growing from 25,000 to 58,000 in the first 60 years of the 20th century — second homes, tourism, and culture were already crowned princes. In the Gilded Age that ended the 19th century, wealthy men collected great estates and built luxury palaces, known as "cottages," some 75 in Lenox and Stockbridge. Major literary figures toured the county: Emerson, Melville, Hawthorne, Holmes, Thoreau, Wharton, Twain. . . . Some settled here. Actors, musicians and artists followed, and are still following.

As the county now, somewhat painfully, recognizes that industries will never again be what they were through World War II, it is coming to rely on a service economy to which, at least, it is no stranger. Filled with fine educational institutions, public and private, with museums and musicians, with art and artifacts to grace the green walls installed infinitely earlier by nature, Berkshire's streams are cleaner and woods thicker than since farms and industry first came to these garrison hills. And the hills retain a plentiful supply of ground water, likely to become increasingly important to the future of this area.

Berkshire has now, as it has had since the ice left, an indigenous population that cares deeply for the land, witness the many towns in the county that have long had zoning, have now established land trusts and are considering land use countywide. Berkshire residents listen attentively at town meetings to discussions of protecting ridges and aquifers, saving farm land, and cleaning up hazardous waste. Little litter mars the many paths. Whether driving its roads or walking its trails, you will soon get the message that this land is cared for.

SOUTH COUNTY

MOUNT WASHINGTON

Mt. Washington, the smallest town by population in the Commonwealth of Massachusetts, has 120 residents. It con-tains 6,500 acres of state land—like the towns of Washington, Savoy, and New Ashford, about one-half state owned. Perched at a 2,000-ft. elevation, like Savoy and Windsor, it is a town formed by its topography. The town may have been settled first as early as 1692 by Dutch moving east from the Hudson River. That would make it the oldest town in Berkshire, but the point is disputed. In any case, the mountain men who lived there about 1730 preferred to consider themselves Bay Colony residents, where individuals owned their land, rather than subject to the feudal tenure of the Hudson Valley. Hudson lord Robert Livingston sent a party onto the mountain in 1755 to extract rents deeded him by the governor of New Amsterdam. A skirmish broke out. Pioneer William Race, for whom Mt. Race and Race Brook were probably named, was killed. In 1761 Livingston's men burned six homes in Mt. Washington. In spite of the fact that the town was incorporated in 1781, the dispute continued until the New York-Massachusetts boundary was settled in 1787.

In the 1840s and '50s inhabitants earned their livings by cutting trees and making charcoal; later, they farmed potatoes; now they drive down off their mountain to work at jobs elsewhere. The scenery is spectacular — a phrase not often used even in a book limited to the best of Berkshire. What a place to begin!

Camping

Part of the charm of Mt. Washington is the absence of any tourist facilities. There is a state-owned cabin on the trail between the two peaks of Alander that can be used on a first-come, first-served basis. The primitive camping area an the Alander Trail is lovely for tenting (no facilities). Camping is available at the New York end of the two-state Bash Bish Park, with facilities. A cabin is available to AMC members (reserved in advance) off East Rd. near Sages Ravine. There are campsites along the AT at Sages Ravine, Bear Rock Falls and Race Brook; a shelter is available just north of Mt. Everett at Glen Brook.

Road approaches

Bear in mind that there are no stores and no gas stations in Mt. Washington. A ski shop, Kenver, is located in So. Egremont. Take Rte. 41 S. from So. Egremont village, but turn right just past the pond, on Mt. Washington Rd. (There is a state forest sign.) After 3 mi., the road swings southerly and begins to climb to a ridge. Signs help at the intersections. The road becomes East St. in the township of Mt. Washington. There is no village center. Pass the entrance to Mt. Everett State Reservation, left, the Union Church, and head straight for Mt. Washington State Forest HQ, right, a complex of brown-stained wooden buildings (9 mi. from So. Egremont). You are about at 1,700 ft., where snow cover is likely to be better than at lower elevations.

CROSS COUNTRY

ASHLEY HILL

Various routes; 2.5-mile trail described. Elevation: 1,500 to 1,800 ft. Intermediate.

You begin on the Alander Trail, which is well marked from the state forest parking lot, where you can register to use the campground. Snowmobiles are not allowed, so that you will have the pleasure of skiing trails that have not been packed. Follow W., from the large map, on the triangular blue blazes the state uses to mark hiking trails, across a field, into the woods, and out into another field. At this point you are virtually on a road, which passes an abandoned house at the bottom of the hill and then crosses Bash Bish Brook on a bridge. Just across the bridge the Charcoal Pit Trail takes off, left, which would make a nice loop with the Ashley Hill Trail, but may not be well maintained.

The Alander Trail crosses another bridge and soon (300 yards from the house) the Ashley Hill Trail, well signed, departs left, beginning a moderate but unrelenting climb. This, too, is wide and smooth, more a woods road than a trail. Six inches of snow on top of some base should cover most of the rocks. The few stream crossings should be frozen, if the weather has been cold. The trail follows Ashley Hill Brook, on your right, offering lovely views down its steep sides. Most of the forest is deciduous, but you pass through some regal hemlock.

How far you go is up to you. You pass a trail to the camping area and the Alander Trail, right, which probably would not make a good loop, because of steepness and major brook crossings. Ashley Hill Trail swings S., eventually passing Brace Mtn. in New York and on into Connecticut. If you go to the Charcoal Pit Trail, entering left, and either take it back or return the way you came, you should have about a 1.25-hr. trip. The downhill ski, on Ashley Hill Trail at least, is significantly faster than the time up, and a thing of beauty.

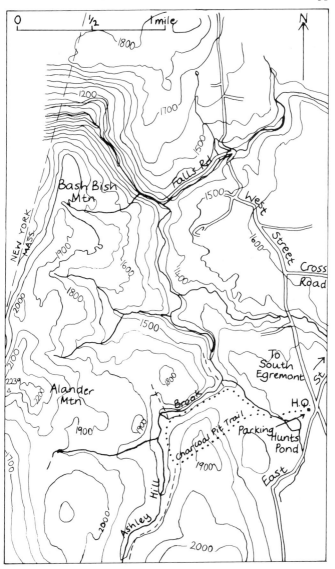

MT. WASHINGTON: ASHLEY HILL

CROSS COUNTRY

MOUNT EVERETT

*5.25-mile round trip. Elevation: 1,700 to 2,602 ft.
Intermediate.*

Road approaches

See "Road approaches" for Ashley Hill, above. The turn, left, to Mt. Everett, off East St., comes a mile before you would reach state forest HQ. If returning from HQ, the turn is right. Drive in the reservation road to the gate.

MOUNT EVERETT

You are just above 1,700 ft. in elevation, and will ski up the road to 2,602 ft. Unlike Greylock, the giant to the N., snowmobiles are not allowed, so diagonal skiers may even find a track made by other skiers.

A gentle grade passes between luxurious laurel growth. In a mile you reach Guilder Pond, at 2,042 ft. The road follows a hairpin turn right, climbing more steeply 1.5 mi. to the end of the road and the stone shelter that faces N. Most skiers make this their destination. The going gets tougher as you follow the access road to the fire tower: quite steep, with sharp corners and a definite potential for ice. This last stretch only extends about .25 mi., however, hikable with skis over your shoulder.

With the foliage off the scrub growth, the view from the summit improves dramatically over that in the summer, in that you can stand in one place and and look nearly 360 degrees. (The fire tower is closed and off limits to the public.) You can get a good view of Alander, to the W.; Mt. Frissel, at 2,380 ft. the highest in Connecticut, to the S.; the Catskills across the Hudson; and most of Berkshire County to the N. (Actually, the state of Connecticut was chagrined to discover recently, as the result of a new survey, that the summit of the "highest mountain in Connecticut" is just over the line in Massachusetts.)

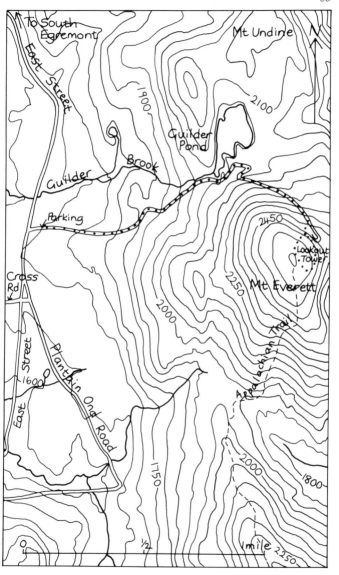

MT. WASHINGTON: MT. EVERETT

On the return, you will probably want to walk most of the way to the shelter. Since the snow is apt to be blown off the ridge, ice may be the biggest problem. The rest of the way back, depending on snow conditions, may be challenging but also exhilarating, with room to maneuver. If conditions cooperate and your knees hold up, you might make it back to the gate in one 10 min. swoop, as opposed to the 45 min. you took on the way up. Round trip will take 1.5 hrs.

SHEFFIELD

The southernmost town center in the county is also the generally accepted oldest (1726), no coincidence when you consider that most of the earliest settlers to Berkshire came from Connecticut. Matthew Noble arrived in 1725, alone, from Westfield, however, to make friends with the natives, clear the land, and erect a cabin. Next he fetched his daughter and returned on horseback to set up the first home in Berkshire (then still part of Hampshire County). The first struggles were not with the Indians but with the New York Dutch, who regarded western Berkshire as their own. In 1735, settlers raised the meetinghouse on Sheffield Plain, a mile north of the present village center.

The first county seat or shire town, when Berkshire became its own county in 1761, Sheffield watched that distinction move gradually north, from Gt. Barrington to Lenox to Pittsfield. Sheffield had its bout with industry, as is true of most Berkshire towns. Distinctively, marble from quarries in Ashley Falls adorns the custom house in Boston and the court house in New York City. Daniel Shays' Rebellion, a movement of Revolutionary War veterans who felt they had been insufficiently compensated for their services, died in battle with government troops in Sheffield in 1789. The town exported its sons.

Chester Dewey trained for four years at Williams College in the fields (literally) in which he was famous in the first half of the 19th century: botany and geology. Another son, Frederick Augustus Porter Barnard, president of Columbia University, determined that Columbia should include women. Barnard College was named for him shortly after he died in 1889.

CROSS COUNTRY

BARTHOLOMEW'S COBBLE

Various trails available; 2 mile route described. Elevation: 664 to 700 ft. Novice to Expert. Donation.

Road approaches

The Col. Ashley House and Bartholomew's Cobble, adjacent properties of the Trustees of Reservations, are S. of the Sheffield town center, near the village of Ashley Falls on the Connecticut line. Turn right on Rte. 7-A, then continue straight, over the railroad tracks, on Rannappo Rd.

BARTHOLOMEW'S COBBLE

The Col. John Ashley House — turn right on Cooper Rd. — is the oldest still-existing dwelling in Berkshire County, built in 1735. Col. Ashley led troops at the Battle of Bennington (1777). The Sheffield Declaration, written there, preceded the Declaration of Independence by three years. Theodore Sedgwick, originally of Sheffield but later of Stockbridge, successfully defended two of the Ashley slaves, Mum Bett and Brom, who sought freedom under a "born free and equal" clause in the state's constitution. That decision led to the freedom of other slaves in the state. The house is open seasonally (not in winter) for guided tours. A trail from it joins the Bartholomew's Cobble trails.

These can otherwise be reached by continuing straight on Cooper Hill Rd. to Weatogue Rd., just a matter of a few hundred yards, to a parking area on the left. A large map of the Trustees' property shows numerous trails. The ones around the Cobble itself, the rocky eminence between the parking lot and the Housatonic River, are shorter and steeper, with some narrow bridges. Bartholomew's Cobble is considered one of the nation's outstanding concentrations of native plants; more than 700 species, including 44 ferns and fern allies, which you'll have to take on faith in January.

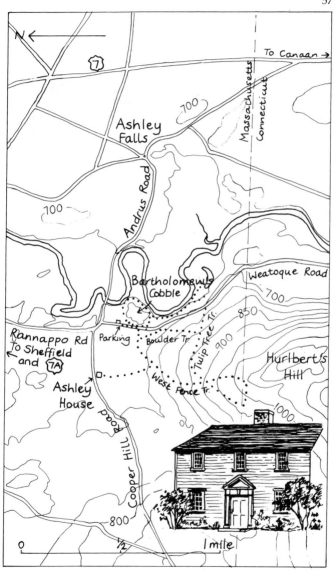

N ←

⑦

To Canaan →

Massachusetts
Connecticut

700

Ashley
Falls

Andrus Road

100

Bartholomew's
Cobble

Weatoque Road

700

850

Parking

Boulder Tr.

Tulip Tree Tr.

900

Rannappo Rd
→ To Sheffield
and ⑦A

West Fence Tr.

Hurlbert's
Hill

1000

Ashley
House

Cooper Hill Road

800

0   ½   1 mile

SHEFFIELD: BARTHOLOMEW'S COBBLE

Trails also range across Weatogue Rd. on open fields and through wooded land. The fields, home to deer and cows, have British-type stiles that enable you to pass where cattle can't. It is possible to ski about 2 mi., generally following white blazes, up the West Fence Trail to the summit of Hurlbert's Hill, from which there is a lovely view centered on Mt. Everett. You can make a loop by returning on the Tulip Tree Trail — although there are some wet spots in mild weather — which crosses Weatogue Rd., and returns you to the maze of trails by the meandering river. You can cover many of the trails in 2 hrs. Return to the Cobble in the spring, when the many ephemeral flowers — those that come out before the leaves on the trees shade them — are blossoming, but before the summer traffic hits.

Not only is the property far S. in the county, it is also low elevation — 664 ft. at the road junction. Therefore, snow conditions may not be as good as elsewhere in the county.

SANDISFIELD

The town of Sandisfield, which has 735 residents, was once so well-to-do that it loaned Pittsfield $40,000 to build its Congregational Church. Time and the railroad passed Sandisfield by, however. The railroad at least left its mark in a stretch of embankment that never had tracks, visible once along Rte. 8. The town was settled in 1750 and became a stop on the Albany to Hartford stage run. In 1902 Solomon Pollack arrived from New York with 35 families who wanted to return to the land. In another influx, Russian Cossacks arrived, settling west of Sandisfield Center. The town took its turn at industrialization, from 1840 to 1870, at which time it boasted 6 taverns and 6 churches. Take your pick. More recently some second-home folks have moved to town but much of it remains a kind of outpost.

CROSS COUNTRY

ABBEY LAKE

3 miles. Novice trail described. Elevation: 1,500 ft. to 1,810 ft. at Abbey Hill summit.

Road approaches

From most of the county, the easiest way to get to Sandisfield is to take Sandisfield Rd. S. from Rte. 23, just E. of Monterey center. Sandisfield Rd. becomes Hubbard Rd. when it crosses the town line, for being in Sandisfield on Sandisfield Rd. would be redundant. Soon turn S. on West St. to arrive at the Abby Hill portion of Sandisfield State Forest. Park at West Lake, on your E.

An alternate approach would be to turn W on Rte. 57 in New Boston, a village in Sandisfield on Rte. 8. Passing through Montville, another village, continue straight on West St., a gravel road, rather than swinging S. on Rte. 57. After 1.5 mi., paving begins as West St. turns N. Soon West Lake Park HQ appears on the right. Park in the lot.

ABBEY LAKE

Want to ski a dam? How about two? This ski in the West Lake, Abbey Lake portion of Sandisfield State Forest gives you a unique opportunity.

High elevation is the key to good skiing in South County. Most of this territory is 1,500 ft., rising to 1,810 at the summit of Abbey Hill. Furthermore, because skimobiles are not allowed, you may find a track laid by other skiers. Ski directly from the parking lot (which is plowed in the winter) or turn right at the gate if you start from the HQ building. Follow the blue-blazed woods road E. In .2 mile the blazed trail turns right, as the Abbey Hill Foot Trail. This narrow route has some steep up and down sections. Experienced skiers may want to give it a try. In 4.5 mi. they will return to the parking lot, following clear blazes around Abbey Lake, to the top of the hill, and then back to the broad road most other skiers will want to ski.

All except advanced skiers should follow that woods road below the West Lake dam and over the outlet brook. Continue right where the road over the dam comes in (ski that route on your return, with this warning: snow cover is likely to be blown or melted off the earth embankment). You head through lovely mixed hardwoods, past the Abbey Hill circuit trail entering left (N.), and ascend the high land dividing the two ponds — which were dammed as part of the Clam River Watershed Project. You start down a wonderful, long curve that brings you out at Abbey Lake and to skiable open fields across its dam.

An alternate route would be to take the Abbey Hill Foot Trail where it departs near the parking lot, which will bring you out to the open field side (E.) of the Abbey Lake dam. There is one steep descent, with a narrow bridge at the bottom, along the way. After crossing the dam, you can return by the road.

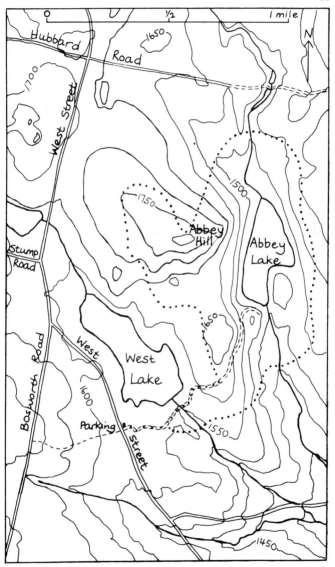

SANDISFIELD: ABBEY LAKE

EGREMONT

Settled in 1730, Egremont is divided into three parts, of which most people only see So. Egremont, an area of an inn, small shops and restaurants along Rte. 23. Egremont Plain and No. Egremont are N., along Rte. 71. The entire town has a population of 1,200.

The area was originally settled by the Dutch in 1730. Prominent landowner Andrew Karner's (Karner's Brook) sister married John Van Guilder (Guilder's Hollow), who was part Indian. No Dutch town name emerged, however; by the time it incorporated in 1760, the town was named for Charles Windham, Earl of Egremont and British Secretary of State. Industry came to Egremont in 1845, when David Dalzel began making axles there, first for carriages and then for automobiles.

The scenic northern end of the Mt. Everett mass, Jug End, juts into Egremont. Commercial development — and skiers — are rising up its side.

DOWNHILL

CATAMOUNT

---

*Trails: 24 (9 Novice, 9 Intermediate, 6 Expert). Summit elevation: 2,000 ft. Vertical drop: 1,000 ft. Lifts: 1 triple chair, 3 double chairs, 1 T-Bar, 1 J-Bar. Snowmaking: 90%. Ski school. Cafeteria. Nursery in separate building. Night skiing on 5 trails. Snowboards allowed. Rte. 23, So. Egremont, on New York State border. **528-1262.***

Catamount is the first good-sized ski area off the Taconic Parkway heading N., and it attracts a New York City and Westchester County crowd, generally families and teenagers, a natural market it has held since its beginnings in the late 1940s. Unpretentious and friendly, Catamount is not a slick resort — not yet, anyway. But there are major changes afoot: the 1990-91 ski season ushered in new lodge facilities and other improvements at Catamount, taking what had become a somewhat shopworn ski area in an upscale direction. Their new high efficiency lighting will make night skiing more attractive,too.

An area to the left of the lodge, not obvious until you ski it, makes Catamount larger than it appears from its entrance. With a vertical drop of 1,000 ft., the mountain offers 24 slopes and trails, most of them rated novice to intermediate. Most have plenty of room to turn, with the exception of Turnpike and Cakewalk, both midmountain crossover routes. You reach the trails by four chairlifts — one of them a triple —, a J-Bar, and a T-Bar. Snowmaking covers 90 percent of the terrain.

The relatively flat, tabletop summit with its 2,000 ft. elevation, offers a view of the county from S. to N. with the twin humps of Mt. Greylock, Berkshire's highest mountain, visible, if the weather is clear, 50 mi. in the distance, almost in Vermont. In the foreground are Monument Mtn., between Stockbridge and Gt. Barrington, and just beyond, October Mtn., jutting up on the E. side of Lenox. From the Ridge Run, just above the chairlift, you can spot Mt. Everett through the trees. Located SE of Catamount near the Connecticut border, Mt. Everett is the highest peak in south Berkshire.

The area's most difficult terrain is to the right looking up from the lodge, with one lift taking skiers to the summit, and the second to just below the summit. The advantage of going to the summit is that it provides access to the intermediate Ridge Run, one of the longer and prettier trails in Berkshire. The summit is unprotected from the wind. You can reach the more difficult trails, Upper and Lower Glade and Dipper and Flipper, by skiing to the left when facing down the mountain from the summit lift, and then dropping down a fairly flat 200 yds. or so to the top of the second lift.

From there, you are poised to leap into the Berkshire panorama by way of the Upper Glade trail. The top is steep and wide, then there's a forgiveness step, followed by another plunge, also wide. From there, the trail descends in a series of more gradual steps. You can avoid the steeper sections by taking the easier Fisher's Fluke, a wind-around intermediate trail that continues as Wax Run to the bottom. Or you can cut back into the less steep Lower Glade that opens into the intermediate On Stage, a wide slope between two chairlifts.

Skiers taking Ridge Run, the easier option from the summit, warm up on a straight but gradual tree-lined run that after about a mile makes an abrupt left turn onto Mountain View, a wide, evenly pitched trail blasted from the mountain in a cut-and-fill operation, leaving a 30-ft. high cliff on the left side, heading down. The lift-serviced Mountain View provides access to a number of easy trails on the east flank of the mountain, or, by staying left, a way back to the lodge. Ridge run to Mountain View is the most enjoyable on the mountain.

If you don't want to ski from the summit right away, you can choose between easy and more difficult terrain that you can see almost in its entirety from the front of the lodge. A new teaching slope is off to the east side of the lodge, where beginning-level classes are out of the way of descending skiers.

Catamount operates a cheerful nursery school in a separate building and a moderately-stocked ski shop. More changes are in the offing, with ambitious plans for a hotel on the New York side and more trail development on the east side.

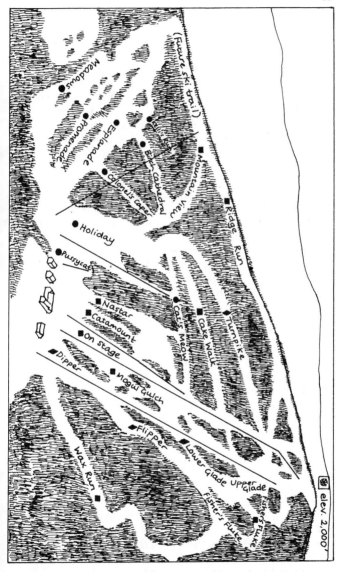

EGREMONT: CATAMOUNT

GREAT BARRINGTON

Gt. Barrington became the focus for southern Berkshire — the shopping center for the hilltowns that surround it, home to a registry of deeds, a court and other status symbols. Nowadays it boasts fine restaurants, theaters, bookstores, a college and numerous other amenities. Along with the center of town, on Rte. 7, there is an old mill area at Housatonic, still home to Rising Paper Co. Originally settled in 1726 at the Great Fordway on the Housatonic, which gave way to the Great Bridge, the town is also on the old Great Rd. from Boston to Albany (roughly Rte. 23 now), so it is no wonder that although named after Viscount Barrington, it magnified the name. By tradition, the Indian village that preceded the town was named Mahaiwe, or "place downstream." A venerable theater in town retains the name.

Back in the days when Americans and British were on the same side, Gen. Jeffrey Amherst, on his way to Ticonderoga, camped with his troops where the Great Rd. crossed the Green River. The town, after separating from Sheffield in 1761, became a seat of discontent with British rule. In August, 1774, a group of men seized the court house, preventing the King's Court from holding session. Thus the town claims the "first open resistance to British rule in America." Yet the town's residents included many Tories — notably leading citizen David Ingersoll, who was imprisoned in Litchfield, Connecticut, and then exiled. British General Johnny Burgoyne marching in defeat from Saratoga on the Great Road during the Revolutionary War, was fêted in Gt. Barrington; during Shays' uprising of dissident veter-ans' the court house was once again seized.

William Cullen Bryant, this country's first native-born poet, practiced law in Gt. Barrington. A poem of his told of an unhappy Indian love affair culminating with her leap from Squaw Peak on Monument Mtn., north of the center of town. A more vivid attempt to explain the cairn or stone pile by the trail records that when the Indian maiden was hurled from the summit, she caught hold of a branch on the way down and remained suspended for two days, howling all the while, until a lightning bolt struck the tree, dropping both maiden and branch to oblivion. Her Mahican Indian relatives built the cairn in her memory, to which passers-by continue to add stones.

In a different application of electricity, William Stanley tested his theory of alternating current by providing street lighting for his home town, the first commercial use of electric current. The Housatonic Agricultural Society and its successors have held a fair at the Barrington Fairgrounds in summers ever since 1842.

Camping

The nearest campground is at Benedict Pond, Beartown State Forest, E. on Rte. 23 to forest HQ. Follow the signs along Blue Hill Rd. from there. The parking fee, charged in season, is modest.

CROSS COUNTRY

SIMON'S ROCK

Several miles of trails. Elevation: 750 ft. Novice.

Road approaches

You can refresh yourself on the W. side of town near the Alford line, beginning at Simon's Rock of Bard College. From downtown Gt. Barrington at St. James Church, drive up St. James Pl., which becomes Taconic Ave. (after the railroad underpass), which becomes Alford Rd. (after curving right). Follow Alford Rd. downhill to Hurlburt Rd., entering left. Park in the lot at the red barns.

To check where you are on a Gt. Barrington town map, locate Hurlburt and Alford roads, the Schweitzer Center farther out Hurlburt Rd. and the midpoint of Round Hill Rd. These points form the rough triangle within which you will be skiing.

SIMON'S ROCK

The barns are the college's Arts Center, called the ARC, pronounced "ark." Inside you will often find a student or faculty show worth a look, avant- or après-ski. You won't see the rock in "Simon's Rock" on this ski: it's a large glacial erratic hidden in the woods on the opposite side of the college, most of which is located across Alford Rd.

The woods off Alford Rd. behind the ARC couldn't be much prettier than on a snowy day. As well as the generosity of nature, consider that of human nature. Elizabeth and Livingston Hall own the large tract of land next to Simon's Rock, which Mrs. Hall founded in 1966. Unlike so many landowners who post forbidding signs to keep out interlopers, for years the Halls have invited the public in, with their nicely wrought signs: "Enjoy, don't destroy." Given the high quality of the cross country skiing through these acres of woods, meadows and fields, you are inevitably inspired to treat the landscape kindly.

Head for the back side of the silo at the rear of the largest barn, skiing downhill toward a small brook and over a narrow bridge. Unless you're the first one out for the day, the track will lead you through a wide open stretch with a riding ring on your left. After crossing a field, you cross the Green River on a hardly noticeable concrete bridge, then another open field — before the real fun begins.

Absorb the mountain views; the biggest mountain, to the S., is Mt. Everett. Ahead lies a combination of woodland trails (bridle-trail wide, revealing summer use) and meadows; the latter usually show well-established tracks around their perimeters. Beginners can do a short loop by stringing together a series of right or left turns. The best glides downhill result from keeping left as you first enter the woods and then circling right a couple of times to come back where you entered. None of the trails is named and there are no maps, but fear not; you'd have to work hard to get lost.

For the more adventurous, a zigzag combination of trails through the woods will lead you to the far corner of the property, diagonally opposite the barn from which you started. From there ski uphill, over cornfield or through woods, until you come out on Round Hill Rd.

The several miles of trails on this unassuming site are a good choice for a 30-min. quicky at either end of work or a more extended aerobic workout.

DOWNHILL / CROSS COUNTRY

BUTTERNUT BASIN

Downhill: Trails: 21 (6 Novice, 9 Intermediate, 6 Expert). Summit elevation: 1,800 ft. Vertical drop: 1,000 ft. Lifts: 1 triple chair, 5 double chairs, 1 Poma. Snowmaking 100%. Ski School with Ski Wee program for ages 4-12. Rentals. Cafeteria. Nursery. No night skiing. Snowboards allowed. Rte. 23, Gt. Barrington, 1.5 mi. E. of town, toward Monterey. **528-2000.**

Cross Country: 7 kilometers of groomed trails. No snowmaking. Rentals. Ski school. **528-0610, 528-2000.**

Imagine a carefully manicured English park that is crisscrossed by well-landscaped paths and then put on an inclined plane. The image that emerges is not far removed from the experience of skiing at Butternut Basin. Try to get there on a weekday, though, because the word is out on Butternut. Weekends, expect a crowd.

Part of the area's parklike feeling derives from its soil and exposure, which encourage the growth of mountain laurel that stays green year-round and lines the sides of many of the trail sections. The colors evoke the feeling of skiing on a path through a green and white garden, a dreamy rush that is pleasantly unexpected.

Butternut was designed and built with love for its surroundings, thanks to hands-on management by owners Channing and Jane Murdock, who bought the abandoned ski area in 1962 and then obtained access to some state land.

Murdock, an ace with a chainsaw and welding torch, maintains a business philosophy that big is not necessarily better, and, conversely, less can be more.

The result is carefully sculpted trails that are mostly easy to ski, yet interesting in a non-threatening way. Although the terrain is generally intermediate, advanced skiers enjoy the views and trail configurations. The two lodges are onsidered models for the industry because of the quality of their appointments, thoughtful signage, and pleasing interior arrangement. Nothing is loud at Butternut; instead, the atmosphere is one of low-key elegance that has attracted a loyal following over the years. *Ski Magazine* presented Butternut with a first place award "in recognition of outstanding environmental planning and excellence of design."

The ultimate Butternut experience is to ride the triple chair on the western shoulder of the mountain. The waiting line forms in a stand of evergreens. As skiers lift off they are almost immediately carried through the grove of evergreens that continues up the mountain from the base, looking down on a mountain stream whose rush is seen and heard through the ice formations. Not until about halfway up does the chair emerge from the woods for a view of the ski terrain.

The summit affords a wide open panorama of the Berkshires, with Monument Mtn. prominently in the foreground. It's a scene that keeps repeating, but thanks to the discreet way the mountain cradles the trails, each view is somehow private.

From the top of the triple, Freewheeler and Downspout offer wide open cruising runs, occasional sharp pitches, and always good run-outs. An alternative way down is via Uptown, an easy start, that connects to Twist for slightly steeper terrain, and finally to Westway, near the bottom for the most challenging part of the ride. This sequence is the most enjoyable on the mountain.

Butternut boasts three other double chairlifts on its main face, one to a three-quarter mark, one to a second summit, and the third serving a beginner area. The first two serve generally intermediate trails that make gentle S-curves as they thread

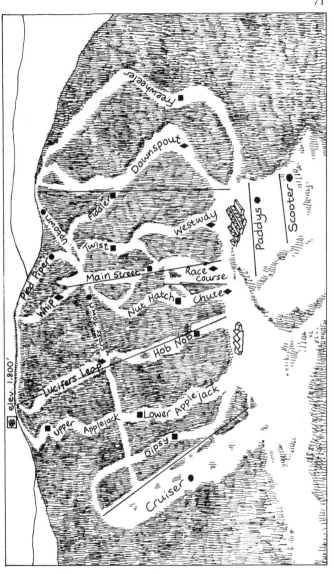

GREAT BARRINGTON: BUTTERNUT BASIN

their way down the mountain, with the most difficult aptly named Lucifer's Leap, for a take-off point near the summit.

The beginner chair on the mountain's east shoulder provides access to a long wide slope and a couple of intermediate trails. Smaller novice slopes, served by two double chairlifts, are in front of the main lodge, completely separated from the more challenging areas.

Conditions at Butternut are among the more reliable in the Berkshires, thanks to 100 per cent snowmaking and a grooming operation that begins when the lifts close in the afternoon and continues through the night, uninterrupted by night skiing.

Einar Aas, one of Berkshire's premier sportsmen, has for generations run a fine ski school here. Active bicyclist, summer camp director, and Josh Billings race organizer, Aas is a local legend.

The area's ski shop has one of the more extensive selections of equipment and skiwear in the Berkshires. Butternut also offers a racing slope for the public's use, equipped with a state-of-the-art coin-operated timing system that displays an instant readout at the finish for each racer. Skiers may race against the clock or another racer on a parallel course.

OTIS

Logically enough, most industry in Otis over the years has been related to wood, for forests did and still do cover most of its land. Thus its reliance on sawmills, woodenware, and tanneries, which used bark in the process of curing leather. Originally called Louden (incorporated in 1773), Otis was settled in the 1750s. Lord Louden commanded American forces in the French and Indian War. Lord Jeffrey Amherst, another soldier of the king, built the Great Road through town in 1759 — approximately Rte. 23 today. In the Revolutionary War, in the winter, Gen. Knox used 124 pair of oxen to tow cannon, captured from Fort Ticonderoga, over this road to Dorchester Heights to relieve the siege of Boston. The road then became known as the Knox Trail. It did not become the Burgoyne Trail, although in 1777 Johnny Burgoyne, the most popular defeated enemy this country has ever seen, marched his men from Saratoga, staying in the Old Inn at Otis. He was fêted almost everywhere he stopped.

Noah Church surveyed the proprietor grants in 1768. Bethlehem, now a part of Otis, was incorporated in 1789; Otis itself, with a population of 1,111, was incorporated in 1810 and named for Harrison Gray Otis of Boston, described by historian Samuel Eliot Morrison as "the urbane Federalist," speaker of the Massachusetts house.

Camping

The second largest freshwater body in the commonwealth, Otis Reservoir (1,000 acres) is mostly in Otis and a hot spot of water sports activity, including camping at Tolland State Forest. The number of second homes is burgeoning by the reservoir and along the Farmington River (Rte. 8). The camping area, containing 5 group sites and 90 tent or trailer sites, is on the peninsula, S. of Reservoir Rd., which joins Rte. 23 in E. Otis with Rte. 8. The campground road is not plowed.

DOWNHILL

OTIS RIDGE

Trails: 8 (3 Novice, 4 Intermediate, 2 Expert). Summit elevation, 1,700 ft. Vertical drop: 400 ft. Lifts: 1 double chair, 1 T-Bar, 1 J-Bar, 1 Pony-bar, 1 rope-tow. Snowmaking: 90%. Ski school. Rentals. Cafeteria. Nursery. No night skiing. Snowboards allowed. Rte. 23, Otis; 13 mi. E. of Gt. Barrington (just off Rte. 8). **269-4444.**

The smallest of all of the Berkshire ski areas, Otis Ridge is a hill in a pocket of wilderness that may well provide more intense instruction for kids than any other Berkshire ski area. Conversely, it won't hold the attention of hotshots or those in search of apres-ski entertainment. The town of Otis is one of the least populated sections of Berkshire County.

The 400-ft. vertical drop at Otis Ridge, with 8 or 9 trails, depending on how you count, means it draws fewer skiers. The potential for one-on-one ski instruction is therefore much better at Otis Ridge than at the more crowded larger areas. And because skiers are never far away from each other instruction often continues even though a particular ski class has ended.

The pacesetter for instruction is the Otis Ridge Junior Ski Camp, since 1948 an institution that is based in a converted farmhouse not far from the summit. The camp, the only one of its kind in New England, operates on the summer formula of bringing kids to a place, then putting them together with enthusiastic counselors to interact in an atmosphere that combines hearty food, spartan living and concentration on a skill. Each weekend during the ski season the camp staff simply adapts these warm-weather ingredients to a winter experience for 60 to 120 youngsters, most of them from New York City, Westchester County, and Connecticut.

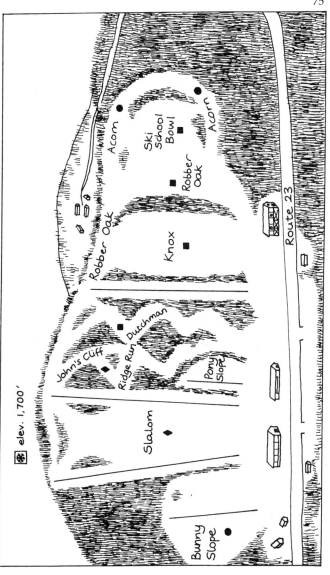

OTIS: OTIS RIDGE

As for the area itself, it's the closest in the Berkshires to the old-style Mom and Pop operations that characterized New England skiing for so many years. The area and the adjoining Grouse House, a lodging and restaurant facility, are owned by two families from Connecticut who draw the core of their help from children, cousins, and miscellaneous relatives. The result is a friendly, informal place best suited for young families.

Although small, Otis Ridge has a surprising variety of terrain. The upper slalom, for instance, boasts a mini-headwall that grows some of the most challenging bumps in the Berkshires. The mogul run is only 50 or 75 yards long but it is wide enough so that you can ski it in dozens of different ways. Skiers who master those bumps are well on their way to proficient skiing on the larger hills. Bumps and Upper Slalom are the most enjoyable runs.

For beginners, the Acorn Trail winds around the W. side of the area, surrounding two small bowls, Knox and Robber Oak. The narrower John's Cliff, Ridge Run, and the Dutchman trails are short and twisty, for skiers who are confident of their turns.

First timers on skis will love the Pony Slope because of its slow-moving, easy-to-grip lift and practically flat terrain. From there they can graduate to the rope-tow-served Bunny Slope and from there to Robber Oak and Acorn for runs from the summit.

MONTEREY

Monterey has a reputation in the county for civic consciousness and environmental awareness. This is a close-knit community of 841 old-timers and newcomers whose amicable communications with each other are facilitated by the *Monterey News*, published by the church. Settled in 1739, once called Green Woods, the town separated from Tyringham in 1847 and was named after a victory in the U.S. war with Mexico. Its factories, in those days, produced paper, rat traps, and cotton.

But its natural resources are its treasure. It contains two lovely lakes, Buel and Garfield— the latter christened in 1894, two days after U.S. President and Williams College graduate James Garfield was assassinated by a crazed job seeker. A sizable portion of the 8,000 acres of Beartown State Forest lies in Monterey, including the beach end of Benedict Pond. The rest of Beartown lies in Gt. Barrington, with a bit in Lee.

Camping

Camping is available at Beartown State Forest along Benedict Pond. There is no parking fee in the winter, but there is a lot of snowmobile and ski traffic. Outhouses and grills are available.

CROSS COUNTRY

BEARTOWN STATE FOREST

Various trails available. Elevation: 1,500 to 2,155 ft. Novice to Expert.

Road approaches

Benedict Pond is the focus of Beartown activity. In the summer you can drive through the park from Rte. 102 in Lee, from the N., but that road is not plowed in the winter.

Most people will arrive at Benedict Pond in the winter by turning N. at the state forest sign on Rte. 23 and left at forest HQ on Blue Hill Rd. After 2 mi., including a stretch of gravel road, turn right (N.) onto a paved park road (.5 mi. to the pond).

BEARTOWN STATE FOREST

The state forest employees have made a determined effort to control whether skiers or snowmobilers (of which there are lots) use a trail. You can pick up a winter-use map of the property, which even shows a separate snowshoe trail. Most of the area is above 1,500 ft., rising to 2,155 on the summit of Mt. Wilcox, so the snow is generally good, as is the hilly terrain.

You can focus your skiing on Benedict Pond, allowing different members of the group to set their own agendas. Warm up some food on a grill in the adjacent camping area.

Numerous alternatives are available, some using routes designated as shared with snowmobiles. Make a choice depending on time, conditions, and stamina. Depending on the state budget, generally on winter weekends park staff is available for recommendations.

The Ski Trail, so-named, which leaves from the W. end of Benedict Pond, is inviting, climbing fairly steeply on the side of Beartown Mtn. (1,865 ft.) and then swinging back to join the Beartown Rd. (shared with snowmobiles), an 8-mile loop for the ambitious. Levi Beebe, Lee's 19th-century weather prophet, lived on Beartown Mtn., using the clarity of the view from there to Mt. Greylock to aid him in his long range prophesies. What do you see? Following the Ski Trail across and to the E. of Beartown Rd. adds 2.0 mi. Shorter loops are available in the Benedict Pond area. It is also possible to ski through the property and out the northern end on trails belonging to Oak N' Spruce Resort (in So. Lee)... and possibly a hot tub. Read on.

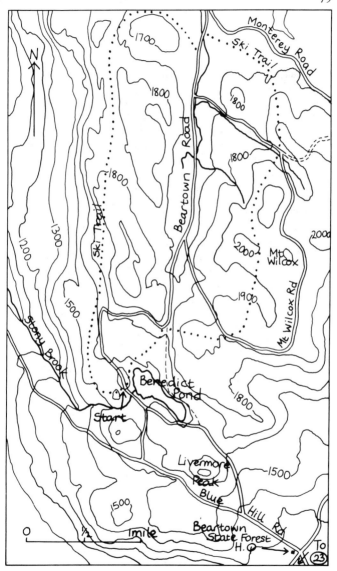

MONTEREY: BEARTOWN STATE FOREST

LEE

Isaac Davis from Tyringham founded Lee in 1760; the town was named in 1777 for Major-General Charles Lee, a hero of the Revolutionary War. A town of multiple ethnic backgrounds, Dutch from New York and English from Connecticut were its first settlers. During the Revolution, an influx of Cape Cod residents of English descent stamped their origin on Cape St. in E. Lee. In the 1860s Italians came to cut marble and then Irish to work on the railroad.

In 1806, Samuel Church built the second (after Crane) paper mill in the county. The Hurlburt Mill came on line in 1822. In 1867, a Lee mill was the first in the county to use wood pulp and in 1891 Eaton arrived to make blotting paper. In midcentury, Charles Heebner of Philadelphia bought a farm and found the vein of marble that is still being mined. Part of Lee went to enlarge the Capitol in D.C., to the headstones for Arlington National Cemetery, to Grant's Tomb, to St. Patrick's Cathedral in New York City, and to the city hall and Girard College in Philadelphia. In Lee itself, the Hydes used local marble in construction of their school.

In a more modest use of marble, a stone in town immortalizes "Highfield Colantha Mooie, a Holstein-Frieson Cow Who Held the World Record for Lifetime Milk Production. Born, lived and died on this farm, 1919-1937." Her total: 205,928.5 pounds.

Levi Beebe, who died at an old age in 1905, lived in what is now Beartown and became well known as a town character and weather prophet. The Beebe Trail in the state forest is named for him.

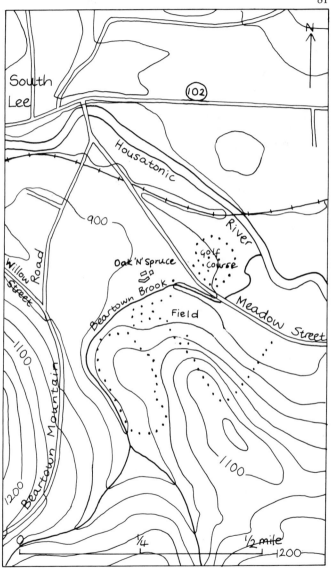

LEE: OAK N' SPRUCE

CROSS COUNTRY

OAK N' SPRUCE

*Various trails under a mile. Elevation: 850 to 1,000 ft.
Novice. Rentals. **243-3500.***

Road approaches

This modest resort, located just off Rte. 102, 2 mi. E. of
Stockbridge and W. of the Massachusetts Turnpike exit,
maintains a half-dozen cross country ski trails in the fields and
wooded area across a small bridge that arches Beartown Brook.

OAK N' SPRUCE

Oak N' Spruce does not charge for the use of the trails
but does offer rentals in its recreation building behind the
main lodge. You can also use the pool, jacuzzi and saunas
for a modest hourly charge, from 10 a.m. to 10 p.m. Whether
skiing there or coming down over Beartown Mtn. to this
destination, the combination of an exercise and a soak sounds
good, and may be unique in the Berkshires, outside of a
major resort. Oak N' Spruce also offers beverages, bathrooms,
and gracious dining as well as accommodations. Why not
have a partner (not quite into the skiing as much as you)
leave you off at Benedict Pond and meet you at the jacuzzi
three hours later?

Due to the relatively low elevation, this will not be your
premier snow spot in the county, but it is an attractive area.
Furthermore, if you follow up the Main Street Trail, you
connect with the N. end of the Beartown State Forest Trail
system, adding another dimension to these skiing possibilities (see the description under Monterey).

TYRINGHAM

The Tyringham Valley remains one of the most lovely, bucolic views in Berkshire. It has stayed that way honestly. No railroad ever came through town, no interurban trolleys nor even a numbered highway. Like Williamstown, it is nearly surrounded by mountains, nestled between October Mtn. and Beartown state forests.

Settled in 1735, Tyringham has always been a farming community, although over the years it has had just a bite of many of the treats served up more extensively in other Berkshire towns. It is the only town in Massachusetts named after a woman, however: Jane Tyringham Beresford, Colonial Governor Bernard's cousin. A handful of Shakers settled here in 1792, growing to a community of 100, cultivating 1,500 acres by mid-19th century when they began to fade. Their land was purchased to build an elaborate summer colony, known as Fernside, on Hop Brook.

Industry arrived in the 19th century, especially the Steadman Rake Company. Richard Watson Gilder, editor of *Scribner's* and later *Century* magazines, arrived in 1898 to build Four Brooks Farm, which attracted the literary and artistic notables of the day, from naturalist John Burroughs to sculptor Augustus Saint-Gaudens to medievalist Henry Adams to humorist Mark Twain — all of whom summered here.

Camping

Tyringham remains free of tourist trappings. There is a campsite, however, available for a donation, at Upper Goose Pond near the AT just over the line from Tyringham in Lee.

CROSS COUNTRY

THE TYRINGHAM COBBLE

*2.0 Miles. Elevation: 1,000 to 1,300 ft. intermediate.
Donation.*

Road approaches

To get to Tyringham from most of the county, go to the
Lee exit of the Mass. Turnpike and proceed on Rte. 102 W,
toward Stockbridge, for a few seconds. Turn left almost
immediately onto Tyringham Rd. A few miles out, turn right
at the town center on Jerusalem Rd. Stay right, where Church
St. enters. Soon you will see a Trustees of Reservations sign,
right, at a natural gas pipeline crossing. Park beside the road
and enter the property through the stile.

THE TYRINGHAM COBBLE

Follow white blazes up an open hillside, through
blackberry and juniper, bearing left at the junction (marked by
a short post)—to which you will return. The trail enters a
wooded area and then comes out on a rocky outlook, where
you may have to remove your skis, the obvious picnic site. The
white church and country town in the Tyringham Valley are
picturesquely set against the wooded hillsides surrounding
Goose Pond. At this point you can decide to return the way
you came or continue on the trail for a circuit.

The trail descends, in some stretches steeply but generally
with room to maneuver, through additional stiles, parallels
the town's main street, and gradually swings right, back to the
trail junction. TTOR owns 206 acres, to which the trail provides
an introduction.

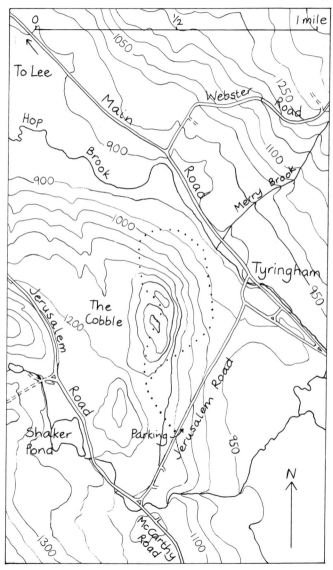

TYRINGHAM: THE TYRINGHAM COBBLE

STOCKBRIDGE

This 250-year-old town (incorporated in 1739) started out chartered by England's King George to "the Housatannack Tribe of Indians . . . to their use and behoof forever." The Europeans who settled there had a notion they could improve the lot of the Indians, however, which led eventually — as it often did — to the Indians being driven out.

The one-armed Rev. John Sergeant, who took the trouble to learn the Mahican language, arrived as first missionary in 1734, teaching Chiefs Konkapot and Umpachene domestic skills like agriculture and house building. His true friendship attracted Indians from many miles away. Jonathan Edwards succeeded him. While well disposed to the Native Americans, he was preoccupied with his religious writings and hectored by those Christian families sent to be worthy examples to the Indians, such as that of Ephraim Williams, Sr. This worthy sold them liquor and connived to acquire their land. So the Indian village became the center of the European town. In 1783 the natives held their last campfire here and migrated to a reservation in western New York State and thence to Wisconsin.

When Judge Theodore Sedgwick moved to Stockbridge from Sheffield in 1785, he stamped the place an important and wealthy town. By the 1860s, like Lenox, it had become the country seat for many influential eastern families. It attracted artists, like Daniel Chester French, who designed the seated Lincoln in the Lincoln Memorial, and Norman Rockwell, the magazine illustrator. It planned well, creating the Laurel Hill Association in 1835, the first village improvement organization in this country, and saving its most precious buildings and historic sites. The Laurel Hill Assoc. is still active, meeting annually, its members planting trees and maintaining trails.

Several of the early and staunch (European) families: the Sergeants, Woodbridges, Williamses, Dwights, Stoddards, Edwardses, Sedgwicks, Fields, Butlers, Choates, Parsonses, Rathbuns, Guerrieris, Burghardts, still have scions in town or nearby. Seven U.S. ambassadors have lived here: Cyrus Field, who laid the Atlantic cable, and his equally remarkable brothers; three men educated here sat on the U.S. Supreme Court at the same time: Henry Billings Brown, Stephen J. Field and David Joshua Brewer. Its recent residents also include the famous and respected, such as psychoanalyst Erik Erikson and theologian Reinhold Niebuhr. And of course one day in the 1960s, according to the song, Officer Obie arrested Arlo Guthrie for throwing some trash from Alice's Restaurant by a Stockbridge roadside.

The town center, which looks like . . . well, a Norman Rockwell *Saturday Evening Post* cover, is the most choked by summer tourists of any Berkshire town. People park a mile out along all the highways to visit the Indian Mission House (the actual building, although not in its original location), the Rockwell Museum, Naumkeag (the Choate mansion, now, like the Mission House, under the care of the TTOR), the many upscale shops and, at the center of things, the Red Lion Inn. A bit farther out, you will find Berkshire Theatre Festival, Chesterwood (the sculptor's home), Berkshire Garden Center and, at the north end of town, the Stockbridge Bowl and Tanglewood (summer home of the Boston Symphony Orchestra).

CROSS COUNTRY

BOWKER'S WOODS

.5 miles. Elevation: 820 ft. Novice.

Road approaches

Go W. on Main St. from the Red Lion Inn, continue straight at the Chime Tower, past the Indian Burial Ground on a knoll to the left, cross the river and bear right up the hill and out Glendale Rd. to a discreet opening in the stone wall, right, for the Lower Trail (1.4 mi. from the inn to trailhead).

BOWKER'S WOODS

The nearly level Lower Trail passes near the loop in the Housatonic and across the freight line and old interurban right-of-way to give you a look at Bowker's Woods. These are largely undisturbed, hardwood, floodplain species. The hardest part is finding the opening in the wall on Glendale Rd. at the start, which doesn't look like a public entrance to anything. Ski through skimpy woods along the path to the railroad tracks. Cross carefully, for you may meet a train. Go straight at the old streetcar roadbed, into thick woods, with the river — including a small island — immediately on your right. The trail wiggles a bit but generally follows the river until turning an abrupt left. Then, the river no longer visible, it continues its wandering ways until it comes out on the trolley roadbed. You turn left and follow the trolley roadbed to the break, right, where the trail comes down from the railroad.

You may want to take another spin or two before crossing the tracks and heading back to Glendale Rd.

Local people are also accustomed to skiing the beautiful Stockbridge Golf Club course, at the W. end of Main St. You can park behind the town hall and approach down the path to the clubhouse, which is closed in the winter. Skiing on the putting greens is forbidden, but the fairways are lovely themselves and offer views of Monument Mtn., to the S. Crisscrossing the Housatonic on the several footbridges is an additional attraction.

Gould Meadows (Rte. 183 and Hawthorne Rd.) and Bullard Woods (near the sharp turn in Hawthorne Rd., E. of Tanglewood's "Lion's Gate") should also provide a happy afternoon of cross country skiing, both under immense trees and across open meadow with dramatic views.

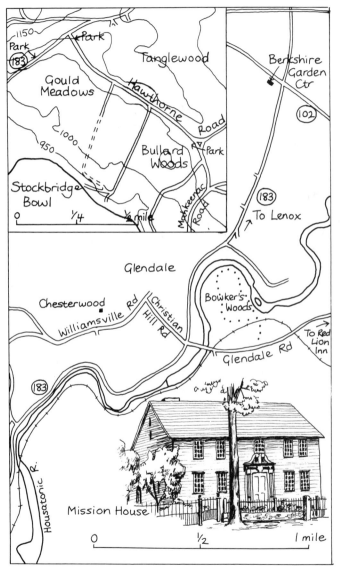

STOCKBRIDGE: BOWKER'S WOODS

CENTRAL COUNTY

BECKET

Becket was number four of four townships established in 1735 by the Great and General Court of Massachusetts.
Joseph Brigham and 59 others moved there by 1740, but
Indian activity drove them out. The first permanent settlement
occurred in 1755 and the town was incorporated 10 years
later. West Becket, where Jacob's Ladder Rd. and Rte. 8
join, was early important as a stagecoach stop, as was the
Bonny Riggs Four Corners. The Becket Center Church, built
in 1780, was thought to have a bell cast by Paul Revere.

One hundred years after incorporation there were 18
sawmills, exporting two million feet of lumber annually and
100,000 bushels of charcoal. As often happened, north, where
the railroad passed, became the main center. In 1927, the
Chafflin-Wheeler Reservoir burst, destroying the town. The
village was rebuilt but never returned to its industrial past.
Today Becket has its share of second homes and summer
camps on Rudd and Center Ponds, as well as the acclaimed
Jacob's Pillow Dance Festival (summer only).

Camping

The nearest public camping is in October Mtn. State Forest,
but on the far side: Lenoxdale. Follow the signs from Rte. 20
either at Lenox or Lee.

CROSS COUNTRY

CANTERBURY FARM

17 kilometers tracked trails: 5 Novice, 2 Intermediate,
3 Expert, plus wilderness skiing. Elevation: average 1,700
ft. Rentals and lessons. Fee. **623-8765**

Road approaches

If you lived in Becket and had a historical turn of mind,
you might name your place Canterbury Farm. After all, Thomas
a Becket (1118?-1170) defied King Henry II from Canterbury
Cathedral. To reach this lodging and cross country ski center,
turn W. on Fred Snow Rd. at the 5-road junction on Rte. 8, N.
of Becket Center. Canterbury Farm is a few hundred ft. up the
gravel road, on the left.

CANTERBURY FARM

David and Linda Bacon, who run the farm, manage over
11 mi. of tracked trails at an average elevation of 1,700 ft.
The system is open to the public as well as overnight guests
who stay in the 1780 farmhouse. David says the trails were cut
for cross country skiing and designed to wander through the
woods for a sense of intimacy, rather than being the broad
avenues of some commercial areas and those designed for the
skating technique.

You get on the trails by crossing a bridge on the S. side
of the farmhouse. This is spruce bog plateau country. On
rolling terrain the trails rise, mostly at moderate grades, from
1,550 ft. to 1,750 ft., offering plenty of snow most of the winter.
The easier trails are closest to the lodge, providing an
unintimidating way in. For a half-hr. loop, bear right on Fox
Trot, past the cabin, straight in the intermediate Tyne Trail
(some moderate grades), which loops back to join Fox Trot,
which crosses a bridge and follows the stone wall through a
spruce plantation back to the start.

As the trails move out in ever larger loops, they take in some steeper sections. From the high point, wilderness trails lead you to Rudd Pond or, the other direction, 11 cross country mi. to Bucksteep Manor.

The farm has been under a forest management plan since the 1930s. The healthy, large, mixed hardwood and spruce plantation show the care. Skiing under their expansive branches is a treat, especially when the snow lies atop.

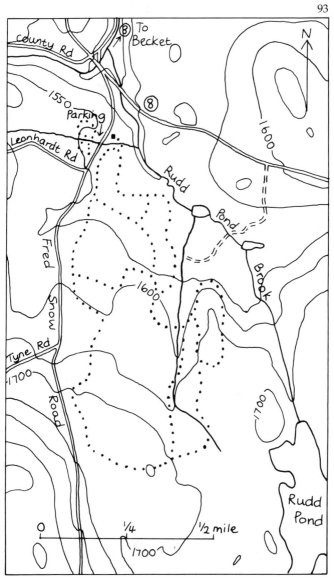

BECKET: CANTERBURY FARM

WASHINGTON

October Mtn. is an evocative name, conjuring up — accurately — a hillside turned multicolor in the autumn. The 14,616 acres of October Mtn. State Forest, visible from Pittsfield and south, provides such a panorama. Most of these acres are in the town of Washington and make up about half of its area, naturally dominating the town. William C. Whitney, secretary of the navy under President Grover Cleveland, put together 11,000 acres of the forest as a vacation colony beginning in 1896. Not only did he have an impressive home there — no longer standing — he also collected a wild animal farm with moose, elk, deer, buffalo, sheep, goats and pheasants, managed by a crew of 55. When the colony closed down the animals were shipped to a New York City zoo. In 1915 the property went to the state. The Schermerhorn Gorge parcel, on the Lenox side, was donated by a Lenox resident.

The town was settled in 1760 by two groups from Connecticut, who called it Greenock. At its incorporation in 1777, the impulse to name it for General Washington was irresistible. The Pontoosuc Turnpike, now Washington Mtn. Rd., also called the Pittsfield Rd., was pushed up and along the plateau in 1830. By the middle of the century, the primary sources of income were mills, some owned by Shakers, and cattle. Now the breadwinners among its sparse population of 602 commute to work in Pittsfield. Like, but not to be confused with, Mt. Washington, in the southern part of the county, Washington has a rugged isolation. Incidentally, there is no Mt. Washington in Mt. Washington, but the range of hills at the N. end of October Mtn. State Forest, in Washington, is called Mt. Washington, as is a brook and two separate roads. Is that perfectly clear?

Camping

Camping is available at the Lenoxdale side of October Mtn. State Forest. Follow the signs from Rte. 20 in either Lee or Lenox to Woodland Rd.

CROSS COUNTRY

BUCKSTEEP MANOR

25 kilometers of trails. Elevation: averages 1,900 ft.
Rentals, lessons, special tours, sleigh rides. Fee. **623-6651**

Road approaches

Bucksteep is on Washington Mtn. (or Pittsfield) Rd. a little S. of town hall. To get to Washington from the S., follow Rte. 8 in Becket N. of Becket Center, where the old church is located on YMCA Rd., and down the hill before the village. At the sharp corner at the bottom of the hill go straight, the middle choice, called McNerney Rd., with Rte. 8 bearing right. After climbing and descending you will rise again to the plateau. McNerney Rd. becomes Pittsfield Rd., a.k.a. Washington Mtn. Rd. Bucksteep is behind the wall on the right. From the square in Pittsfield, go E., bearing right at the fork, on Elm St., which flows into William St. Cross Division St. and bear right on Washington Mtn. Rd.

BUCKSTEEP MANOR

Bucksteep was built at the turn of the 20th century on the model of an estate in England, even to the Episcopal Chapel you see by the road. David and Tricia Drugmand lease facilities from the owners of Bucksteep Manor, a separate operation, to run the cross country skiing. Swing around the manor house to the rental building beside the parking lot. The 25 km. of trails, which depart from the rental shop, are fairly evenly divided among Novice, Intermediate and Expert, over relatively level territory at 1,900 ft. elevation and above. Snow cover is dependable at this elevation, the highest of any commercial center in the Berkshires.

For starters, you might try Pine Run, a novice loop to the S. of the rental shop. It begins in open fields, but soon winds among young growth, including, of course, pine. After the bridge, turn sharply left at the trail junction. You pass another trail junction before returning to the open fields behind the rental shop, some 15 mins. later.

Trails are groomed for both diagonal and skating techniques. Rental and repair are available, as well as a lounge with liquor license in the barn. The barn offers nightclub-style entertainment on weekends. Meals and lodging are available in the manor, as well as rustic camping in cabins. Instruction is offered along with special events, such as moonlight skis and races. High schools' cross country meets are held at Bucksteep. Snowmobiles are not permitted.

Guided ski tours can be arranged to October Mtn. State Forest, just across the road (see the October Mtn. description).

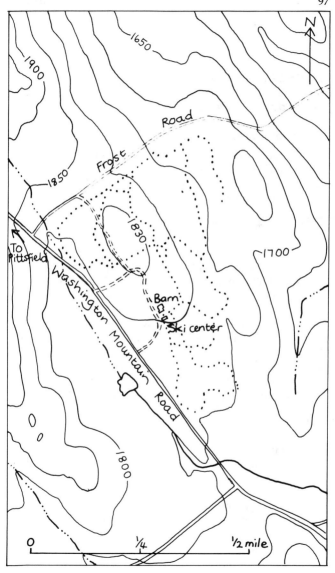

WASHINGTON: BUCKSTEEP MANOR

CROSS COUNTRY

OCTOBER MOUNTAIN STATE FOREST

Various distances. Elevation: 1,900 ft. Novice.

Road approaches

Numerous access points exist, but probably the easiest is West Branch Rd., just N. of Bucksteep Manor and across Pittsfield Rd. (by the Washington town common). See directions to Bucksteep, above.

OCTOBER MOUNTAIN

This, the largest of Massachusetts' state forests, has a wealth of unplowed roads heavily used by snowmobilers and some trails, notably the Appalachian Trail, that belong to skiers in the winter. West Branch Rd., unplowed, is snowmobile heaven; yet, broad and rolling, it's a good novice ski. Some .5 mi. in (W.) and down, trails intersect: first, a yellow blazed one, left, which in 2.0 mi. takes you to Watson Rd. and thence back to the main road. Second, you can ski either N. or S. on the AT, a few hundred ft. farther in, at a brook. It is designed as a hiking trail; however, narrow and twisty for skiing: N. will return you to the main road in 1.25 mi.;. S. will take you on a longer loop, 4.0 mi. back to the road (keep bearing left) via Watson Rd. In either case you could ski along the side of the road back to your car.

If you ski on West Branch Rd. for 2.0 mi. you come to its intersection with (also unplowed) Whitney Place Rd., opening up a network of skiable roads. If you go straight ahead at the 4 corners for another .5 mi., you come to a splendid destination: Washington Mtn. Lake, a reservoir and good picnic spot. The elevation at the lake is 1,798 ft., about 150 ft. lower than the starting point. The dike provides some wind protection.

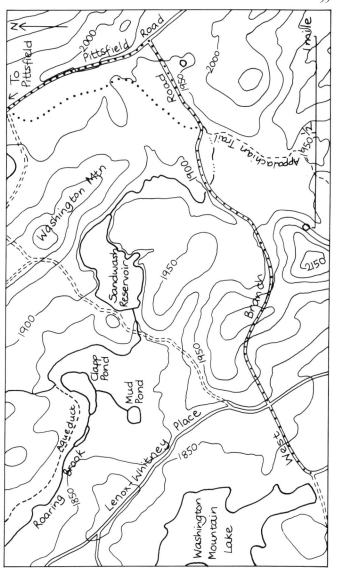

WASHINGTON: OCTOBER MOUNTAIN

LENOX

Lenox is not at all what you see from Rte. 7, a strip of shops and restaurants. The old center of town is on Rte. 7-A; that, too, has a touristy inclination but is recognizable as a community with a rich history.

Originally connected to the outside world only by an Indian path that followed the Housatonic River, Yokuntown was first settled in 1750 and named after Chief Yokun, a Stockbridge Indian. When the town was incorporated, in 1767, it was named for Charles Lennox, Duke of Richmond. At some time, one *n* was deemed sufficient; the opposite of the inclination that added "great" to Viscount Barrington's name. Considered a home to Tories during the Revolutionary War, by early in the 19th century its thriving industries led it to replace Gt. Barrington as the shire town: hence the court house (1816), now the Lenox Library. Pittsfield usurped the county seat in 1868.

Lenox changed utterly, however, when Charles Sedgwick moved there in 1821. Shortly thereafter, his sister, writer Catherine Sedgwick, joined him. Together they hosted the literary lights of the day and inspired other families to build great estates in town, the so-called cottages designed on the Newport, Rhode Island, model. Many well-to-do gentry from New York and Boston developed large estates in and around Lenox, tastefully tucking their enormous homes out of sight behind shrubbery. Few of these remain in private hands now. The most famous visitor at the time was the British actress Fanny Kemble, who charmed the community and to whom Longfellow addressed a sonnet. She donated the proceeds of a reading to pay for the clock in the tower of Lenox's lovely Church on the Hill.

CROSS COUNTRY

KENNEDY PARK

Various trails; 2.5 miles as described. Elevation: 1,400 ft.
Novice to Intermediate.

Road approaches

A history of large estates — as opposed to farm land, cutover land, or developed land — has left some of the largest trees in the county in Lenox and Stockbridge, as you can see in Bullard Woods or driving through these fashionable towns. One gorgeous glimpse of the kind of land that is not recently grown over farm fields is Lenox's Kennedy Park. Best access is from the Church on the Hill, well within walking distance of downtown, or from the parking lot near the junction of Rtes. 7 and 7-A.

KENNEDY PARK

The park accommodates a range of skiing abilities. The area was the site of the Aspinwall Hotel, built in 1902 to house the wealthy who wanted to visit their cottage-dwelling friends. The hotel burned in 1931 and its grounds became the John D. (not John F.) Kennedy Park in 1957. The main trail, blazed white and suitable for novices, breeds numerous offshoots, so that you can design your own route. Other trails are mostly intermediate. Scenic lookouts as well as powerline cuts provide nice views. Powerline cuts are also skiable, although rougher than the trails.

One possible tour begins at the Church on the Hill and enters the park at the entrance slightly uphill. This drive is plowed to the water tower, but you can ski alongside it. A sign notes that you are benefiting from trail grooming for the Lenox Memorial High School cross country ski team. A larger sign shows the trail layout. At the fork beyond the tank, bear left to a lovely view on a terrace, W. and S., including Mt. Everett. At the next junction you can make a loop, which will turn into a figure 8, with the Lookout Trail, left, to the main trail and back.

Or you can ski all the way along the main trail to its end at Reservoir Rd., close to Massachusetts Audubon's Pleasant Valley Sanctuary. More about that anon.

LENOX: KENNEDY PARK

CROSS COUNTRY

PLEASANT VALLEY

Various routes. Elevation: 1,340 to 2,126 ft. Novice.
Fee for non-members.

Road approaches

Unless you ski to Pleasant Valley Wildlife Sanctuary
through Kennedy Park, you will probably drive to it from the
Lenox-Pittsfield Rd. (Rtes. 7 & 20). Turn W. on W. Dugway
Rd., at the sanctuary sign, N. of the junction with Rte. 7-A but
S. of the junction with Holmes Rd. Follow Dugway 1.0 mi.
until it ends at W. Mountain Rd. Bear left for .8 mi. The
sanctuary, which is closed Mondays, has parking areas on
both sides of the road.

PLEASANT VALLEY

Pleasant Valley was established in 1929. Winding through
1,100 acres of beaver swamps and wooded uplands are 7
mi. of trails, and at the present time a 1-mi. loop trail is
open for skiing. Cross country skiing is permitted Tuesday
through Sunday until 4 p.m.   Maps and other interesting
pamphlets are available at the window, where non-
members of Massachusetts Audubon are asked to pay a
small fee for the use of the Sanctuary. Dogs are not allowed.
Many trails are open to foot travel only, including
snowshoes, which the sanctuary rents to visitors for on-
site use. Cross country skiing is not permitted on these
trails. All trails heading away from the administration
building are blazed blue; all returning to the center are
blazed yellow; cross trails are blazed white. It is difficult
to get lost.
Trails along the ponds and Yokun Brook are accessible
to anyone, and are both lovely and interesting. Start by
following the main drag, Bluebird Trail, by the Trailside
Museum and down a gentle slope to the bridge over Yokun

105

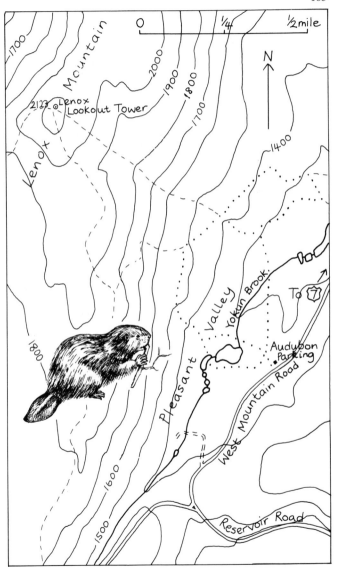

LENOX: PLEASANT VALLEY

Brook. You travel through fields in which trees are just beginning to reestablish themselves. Cross the bridge, into the tall pines, and follow Beaver Loop around a set of wetlands and back on the Yokun Trail.

Legally, wetlands are defined not only by water but by the sedges (grasses), red osier dogwoods (which look red even in the winter) and other plant species. Did you think beavers were dormant in the winter? You probably can find some evidence of chewing, which you may have interrupted. The best place for a trail picnic is probably the open fields near the Trailside Museum (closed in winter).

PITTSFIELD

Solomon and Sarah Deming arrived from Wethersfield, Connecticut, at what's presently Elm St. and built their first home in 1752. They were Pontoosuc's first European settlers and their daughter, Dorothy, the first child of European extraction born in this wilderness. The other earliest residents were also from Connecticut, which was true in much of western Massachusetts. Settlers gathered in sufficient numbers over the next year to discuss founding a town and building a meeting house, located beside what became Park Square. They decided to name the town for William Pitt, English statesman who befriended the colonies and whose birthday was the same as the day in April, 1761 that Berkshire County split off from Hampshire County. Pittsfield was to become the shire town or county seat of Berkshire.

In 1764, Rev. Thomas Allen became the first minister, later accompanying the troops to the Battle of Bennington (1777), as the "Fighting Parson." The elm next to the first meeting house was spared in the construction of the second church, the one Charles Bulfinch designed, by the intercession of Lucretia Williams, who spent an altogether interesting few decades. Loyal to the king like her father, Israel Williams, she married the ardent patriot John Williams (no relation; every fourth person in western Massachusetts in those days was named Williams). Yet she survived and their marriage survived. At least they had plenty to talk about, and in 1783, when the peace was signed, they threw a party that, judging from contemporary accounts, may scarcely have been equaled since.

The elm, although struck by lightning, lived into the days Herman Melville spent in Pittsfield. He described scarred Capt. Ahab in terms of that tree, "greenly alive but branded." It finally had to be removed in 1864.

Poet Oliver Wendell Holmes' great-grandfather, Jacob Wendell, who originally bought the land for Pittsfield in 1736, drove a wonderful "one-hoss shay," subject of the poem "The Deacon's Masterpiece." That shay now sits in the basement of the Berkshire Museum, on South St., together with many other artifacts from the city's literary, historic, natural, and artistic past. O.W. Holmes's property is now owned by the Massachusetts Audubon Society, called as it always has been, Canoe Meadows. It is located where Pomeroy Ave. meets Holmes Rd.: Holmes Rd. being also the address of Melville's Pittsfield home, "Arrowhead" — now the headquarters of the Berkshire County Historical Society. The poet Henry Wadsworth Longfellow, of "Hiawatha" fame, stayed at the Dutch Colonial mansion built in 1781 by Henry Van Schaack, now the Pittsfield Country Club.

This building on Rte. 7, south of town, originally known as Broad Hall, was also the home for nine years of Elkanah Watson, who married science with agriculture in Berkshire. The merino sheep he imported changed the nature of farming in the county; the agricultural fairs he founded still continue in some form or other throughout western Massachusetts.

Another application of science created the modern city, which in the 19th century was smaller than its North County rival, No. Adams. In 1907 the General Electric Company established its plant in Pittsfield. A city that took 150 years to gain a population of 25,000, doubled that in the next 30 years. (And continued growing to near 58,000 in 1960. It has declined since.) GE, still active in Pittsfield, continues to manufacture electrical parts, although emphasizing plastics and ordnance now.

Early industries used water for paper and waterpower. As well as drawing from the Housatonic River and its tributaries, industries enlarged two lakes, Onota and Pontoosuc, as water reservoirs. Both now serve as recreational bases. Public swimming is available at Burbank Park on Onota and at the park just off Rte. 7 on Hancock Rd. for Pontoosuc. A city of nearly 50,000 once more, 36 percent of the entire county, Pittsfield is refreshed by its lakes and keeps its eye on the hills that surround it.

CROSS COUNTRY

BERRY POND

*5 miles of trails as described; other trails available.
Elevation: 1,245 to 2,060 ft. Intermediate.*

Camping

Pittsfield State Forest has two campgrounds. The one at Parker Brook, to the W. of the HQ, has 18 sites. The one at Berry Pond, your destination, has 13 sites.

Road approaches

From Park Sq., Pittsfield, follow W. on West St., 2.5 mi.; turn right on Churchill St. for 1.25 mi.; and left at the chocolate-colored state forest sign on Cascade St. .5 mi. to the state forest entrance. From the N., turn right on Bull Hill Rd. off Rte. 7 in Lanesborough and go .5 mi.; jog left and then right on Balance Rock Rd. Turn right on either Hancock Rd. or Causeway and then left on Churchill to Cascade; right at the state forest sign from which it is .5 mi. to the parking area at Lulu Pond and the end of the plowed road.

BERRY POND

There are many trails in the forest you may wish to try out. The 5.0 mi. loop on Berry Pond Circuit Rd. can be seen as the basic ski tour, suitable for intermediates, with the other trails as elaborations. It includes the most remarkable view in the forest and passes by Berry Pond, at 2,060 ft. in elevation the highest natural body of water in Massachusetts. This book recommends making the tour clockwise, against the likely flow of any snowmobile traffic and in order to climb the steepest sections while enjoying the longer, more gradual downhill.

Ski back to the unplowed road heading W. Ski up and over a low divide to come out on what would be, in season, the downhill section of Berry Pond Circuit Rd., .5 mi. from the lot. You will now ski fairly steeply uphill for 2.0 mi., with occasional views to the S., over Parker Brook. You won't know it, but you cross the town line into Hancock. The Taconic Skyline Trail enters from the S.; as you come down around a curve, Berry Pond will be on your right (E.). You might like to ski through the camping area, beside the pond.

From now on, as they say, it's all downhill. You ski through the azalea fields that are so fragrant in late spring. You are probably more aware of the stiff, cold breeze, however. As you round a corner, to the W. a wonderful overlook into New York State open before you. Then the Taconic Skyline Trail, blazed white, continues straight while the road swings E. You may be entering a period of prolonged snowplow position, if the snowmobiles have packed the road and it has iced, because from here on, the road is more or less a straight, 2.0-mi. shot to where you left your car, with Lulu Brook on your left. With some luck, however, you'll find powder beside the snowmobile track, or you may want to take a left on a major trail a few hundred yards beyond the Skyline Trail, down a steep but short bank, cross the brook, and right on the Honwee trail back to Lulu Pond.

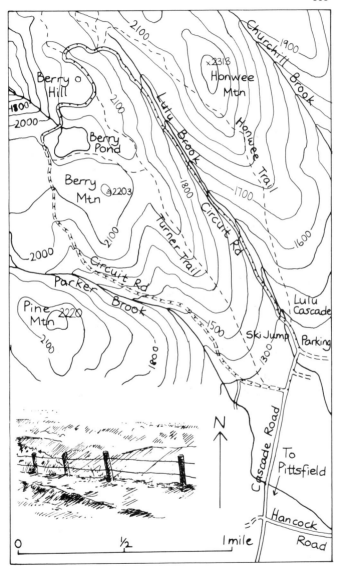

PITTSFIELD: BERRY POND

CROSS COUNTRY

CANOE MEADOWS

Various trails available. Elevation: 950 ft. Novice. Donation.

Road approaches

This Massachusetts Audubon Sanctuary consists of 262 acres of wetlands bordering the Housatonic River. Access is from Holmes Rd. just to the N. of its junction with Pomeroy Ave.

CANOE MEADOWS

The property, with its 3.0 mi. of trails, is open 9 a.m. to dusk, Tuesday through Sunday. Snowmobiles and dogs are not allowed on these ungroomed trails. The foliage filters the sound of traffic and the sights of nearby homes, so that although you are in a residential area, the property carries you to the open fields of an earlier Pittsfield. No rest rooms or other facilities are available. The essentially level trails across meadows and occasional bridges are skiable as long as wet areas are frozen under the snow. You can see where you are going and where you have come from pretty much at any point in this largely open area. There is a self-guided nature tour.

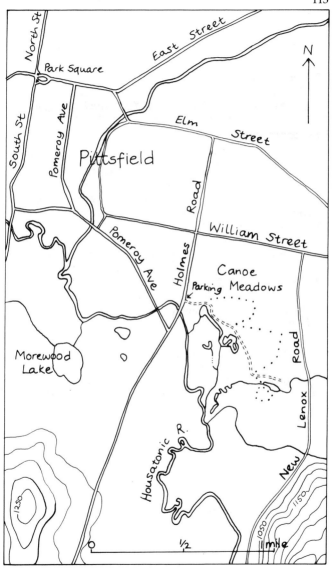

PITTSFIELD: CANOE MEADOWS

CROSS COUNTRY

KIRVIN MEMORIAL PARK

Various trails available. Elevation: 1,000 ft. Novice.

Road approaches

From Park Sq. in Pittsfield drive out East St. At the fork, bear right on Elm St., which brings you into Williams St. Look right at 3.5 mi. from the Sq., just after Juliana Dr., right, and across from Pine Grove Dr., left. (If you get to Burgner's Turkey Farm, at the Division St. junction, you've gone a bit too far.) Turn in at the sign that says "Dr. Robert J. Kirvin Memorial Park." Park along the road or in a cleared lot by the playing fields.

KIRVIN MEMORIAL PARK

Park along the road or in a cleared lot by the playing fields. Boy Scouts have cleared and marked 4.0 rolling mi. of trails in the area of Sackett Brook, straight ahead, beyond the athletic fields. The trails are not groomed. Like Canoe Meadows, this area is within easy distance of thousands of people, who might otherwise be tempted to drive for miles to find a place to ski. Like Canoe Meadows, you should choose your own route. Even in the wooded section, the brook serves as a reference so that you won't get lost.

DOWNHILL

BOUSQUET

Trails: 21 (6 Novice, 7 Intermediate, 8 Expert.) Summit elevation: 1,875 ft. Vertical drop: 750 ft. Lifts: 2 double chairs, 3 rope tows. Snowmaking 100 %. Ski School, Ski Shop, Rentals, Cafeteria. Night skiing on 13 trails. Snowboarding allowed on all trails. **442-8316**

The senior among the Berkshire ski areas, Bousquet was founded in 1932 using a hill on the Clarence J. Bousquet farm. Skiers climbed up to ski down. By 1935, however, Bousquet had engineered the greatest ski promotion of the time by arranging for snow trains from New York City carrying skiers for $3 a round trip. For an extra $1 they could use the rope tows that by this time Bousquet had installed on his hill.

Skiing has changed considerably since then and instead of catering to New Yorkers, Bousquet now draws primarily a Pittsfield area crowd, thanks to snowmaking, night skiing, and an extensive racing program that is ideally suited to the contours of the hill. With a vertical drop of 750 ft., Bousquet is not large, yet offers a surprising amount of skiing on about 8 major trail systems that are collectively dubbed by the area as "the best kept secret in the Berkshires."

The secret is beginning to get out, however, particularly among members of the second-home community in the Berkshires, a group whose ranks swelled during the 1980s. Its summit elevation of 1,875 ft. affords a majestic view. The summit looks down on the city of Pittsfield and N. to the twin humps of Mt. Greylock and W. to the Taconics.

The area offers a choice of 2 double chairlifts, one going three-quarters of the way to the top, and the second to the summit, and 3 rope tows serving ski school and beginner areas.

The summit is a knob, representing the steepest part of the mountain, with a choice of 4 short ways to descend

— 3 of them stretches with challenge and one an easier ride. From the bottom of the knob to the base, it's wide open skiing over pitches and bumps but nothing too steep for intermediates. The most enjoyable run: Easy Rider to Grand Slalom.

On windy days, you can avoid the summit by taking the much easier runs that spread out from the top of the T-Bar and three-quarters-of-the-way-up chairlift. They provide access to the wide open Grand Slalom and Main Street trails, the smaller East and Russell Slopes and the thoroughly delightful Drifter, a novice trail that winds around the S. side of the mountain.

You will note that skiers are pretty good at Bousquet. The area sells a lot of season tickets to those of school age. Graduates from the Bousquet slopes include Heidi Voelker of Pittsfield, a member of the 1988 U.S. Olympic Team; twin sisters Kim and Krista Schmidinger of Lee, likely Olympic team members; and Nancy Gustafson of Pittsfield, a winner in the World Disabled Championships. All are children of ski instructors in the school operated for more than 25 years by Court McDermott of Pittsfield and Rick Latimer of nearby Richmond.

Bousquet's lodge, although in need of sprucing up, affords an attractive bar area and lounge on its upper floor that opens out to a deck overlooking the trails. Cafeteria, ski shop and ski rentals are below. First-timers have their own little area, fenced off between the two chairlifts and served by a short rope tow. On weekends, when other areas are crowded, Bousquet is a good bet because of its limited marketing.

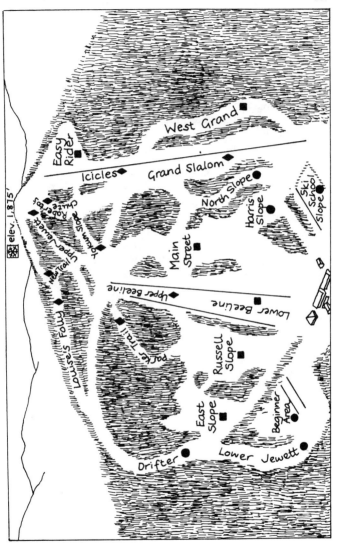

PITTSFIELD: BOUSQUET

HANCOCK

On the map, Hancock looks like what was left over maybe when the rest of Berkshire County was laid out: a long, narrow strip along the northwestern boundary of the county and thus the state, running from Williamstown to Richmond. It is impossible to drive from one end of Hancock to the other within the town lines. Six thousand acres of mountainous Pittsfield State Forest intervene. The three sections of the town of 800: north, village, and Shaker, draw mail from different post offices, draw wires from different utilities, and pledge different loyalties.

Settled in pre-Revolutionary times, the town was originally called Jericho, because the steep slopes were likened to the walls Joshua sent tumbling. When it was incorporated in 1776, it was named for the patriot whose large signature decorates the Declaration of Independence, John Hancock. Samuel Hand, who represented the town in the state government in the 1790's, asked his fellow lawmakers for hazardous duty pay — or at least a clothing allowance — because "the mountains are so steep that one can not climb out without spoiling the knees of his pantaloons, or go back without spoiling his seat."

The biggest business by far is Jiminy Peak, once solely a ski area and now a mountain resort. The second largest business is the not-for-profit Hancock Shaker Village. Second home developments are rising. A few farms, a few stores, some bed and breakfasts and restaurants, as well as the more commercial area along Rte. 20 out of Pittsfield, make up the rest of town.

CROSS COUNTRY

SHAKER MOUNTAIN

3.5 mile trail. Elevation: 1,200 to 1,845 ft. Intermediate.
Grounds fee.

Road approaches

Because Hancock Shaker Village is at the southern extremity of the town, the easiest way to get there from anywhere in the county is through Pittsfield. From Park Sq., follow Rte. 20 west for 5 mi. Park in the lot on the S. side of the road.

SHAKER MOUNTAIN

Shaker Village is only open for a few special occasions in the winter, but since you will be starting your ski on village property, it would be considerate to check in at the office, next to the parking lot, where there are apt to be people on any working day. There is a $5 grounds fee. You should plan to return to tour the village, if you have not already done so, from May to October, 9:30 a.m. to 5 p.m.

The Shaker religion reached its zenith in this country in the 1830s. These celibates believed that all work was an expression of God's glory; they also continued styles of the 18th-century time of their sect's founding. Thus their furniture and craftsmanship are both simple and exquisite. A tour of 20 restored buildings, including craft workshops and the famous round barn, takes at least 2 hours. There is a fee.

This ski takes you past the unrestored remains of the North Family or industrial grouping of Hancock Shakers. Included is the village water system, mill sites, dams, the foundations of a residence, 150-year-old cart roads, charcoal-burning sites, stone walls, and its hilltop holy site.

Cross Rte. 20 to the fields behind the 1793 meetinghouse. Strap on your skis; you're starting at elevation 1,200 ft. Head N. to the logging road. The trail departs N. from a cleared log landing a couple hundred yards from the highway. It is maintained and signed by Boy Scouts, but the signs probably aren't there in the winter. Begin on the cart road that soon follows the western side of Shaker Brook. The stone walls may have been laid up in 1845. Soon you arrive at the lower dam, the beginning of a sophisticated water system. The pipe fills a reservoir you passed (but may not have noticed), from which it traveled underground to the village where it first powered machinery, then supplied the washrooms, then the stables, then the mills, and then the fields to water the cattle. Since the old bridge is washed out, look for a likely place to cross the brook. You will have to take off your skis.

Follow down the eastern side (retracing your steps but on the other side) of the stream, passing first an industrial site with a pit for a water wheel and then the cellar hole for the North Family residence. To imagine its size, compare it with the Brick Dwelling in the village, although this one was made from wood. The trail turns left, up the hill, through second-growth hardwood with some shagbark hickory and hemlock, on what was probably the Shakers' original cart road to their Holy Site. Bear left where a branch of the road continues straight. This was a charcoal-burning site. Cross under power lines that serve airplane beacon lights for the Pittsfield airport; switch back and cross under them again. This is a loop with a steep ascent and a long, gentle descent.

At 1.75 mi. you enter the overgrown field that was the Hancock Shakers' holy ground, on what they called Mt. Sinai, now referred to as Shaker Mtn. (elevation 1,845 ft.). The Shakers did not permit non-believers on this site. In 1841 or 1842, all Shaker communities were required to clear the summit of a nearby hill, focusing on a "fountain" or hexagonal fence surrounding a marble slab, about which they marched, sang, and danced in May and September. The Lebanon community's holy ground, called Holy Mount, is about a mi. northwest as a bird flies. Shakers called to each other across the chasm.

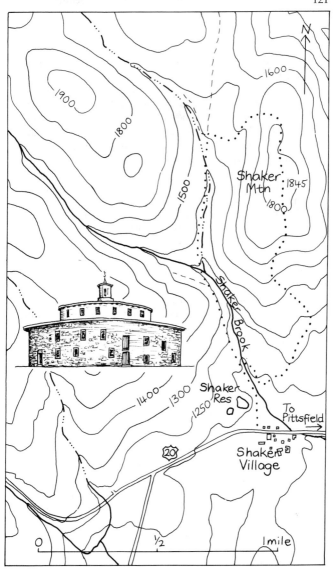

HANCOCK: SHAKER MOUNTAIN

The trail follows the ridge on a fine, rolling, wooded section to ski, gradually losing altitude, and then turns left, into the valley, with some short steep and narrow sections. It switches back through a hemlock grove (some vestigial red blazes remain in Pittsfield State Forest land). At the bottom of the hill, in a low growth, swampy section, turn left on the lumber road, which is an extension of the road on which you started out. The road that turns right almost immediately would take you to Holy Mount, but it is not skiable — the carting road back in is, eminently: 2.0 mi. worth.

As you lose elevation through a cutover section of forest, you approach the main stem of Shaker Brook, which you must ford. You may have to remove your skis. Continue on the cart road, crossing a much smaller branch of the brook and passing the Holy Mount trail, which comes in from the W., at the site of the high dam. It may have been constructed in 1810. When it was whole, it must have created a large pond; now it is washed out. Just below, the Shakers built a sawmill that bridged the stream. Logs were loaded at the retaining wall on the far side. This mill, which ran on water power — or steam, when water wasn't sufficient — was built mid-19th century and burned in 1926.

Follow the cart road to the log landing, leaving the reservoir in the raised land on your right, and back to Rte. 20.

DOWNHILL

JIMINY PEAK

Trails: 25 (35% Novice; 30% Intermediate; 35% Expert). Summit elevation: 2,390 ft. Vertical drop: 1,140. Lifts: 1 triple chair, 3 double chair, 1 J-Bar. Snowmaking: 95%. Ski school, Ski shop, Rentals, Two cafeterias, Nursery. Night skiing on 13 trails, or 86% of skiable terrain. Snowboards allowed. **738-5500**

Jiminy Peak, Berkshire's only 4-season ski resort, offers the county's most challenging runs for advanced skiers. The combination of the terrain and resort amenities makes skiing Jiminy feel more like skiing in Vermont, New Hampshire and Maine.

Like other areas in the county, Jiminy has trails for everybody, cafeteria facilities, a ski shop and rental operation. But it also has an upscale restaurant, a trailside tavern, trailside condominiums, townhouses, tennis courts, a trout pond, and a golf putting course. The facilities are housed in a collection of handsome buildings, including a 105-room condominium hotel, clustered at the base. The architecture is understated; nothing shouts. In June 1990, the way all of the elements fit together at Jiminy was recognized by *Snow Country Magazine*, which chose the area for its "Overall Resort Design" award for resorts of its size.

First and foremost, however, Jiminy is a ski area that has evolved steadily since its humble opening in 1948, with one T-Bar (the first in Massachusetts) that went halfway up the mountain. Today Jiminy Peak is a full scale ski resort with a commitment made to lay down new snow just about every night and then groom it to perfection for the 9 a.m. milk-run enthusiasts. In addition there's skiing every night with about half the trails lighted and a serious commitment to teaching and encouraging racing programs. On weekends it will be crowded.

Beginners will like the J-Bar area because it's tucked away from the crowds. They will also like the open slopes right in front of the Crane Lodge where they can ride a short chairlift to show their stuff with plenty of room to make turns and no unpleasant surprises from the terrain.

Intermediates riding the triple to the 2,390-ft. summit have the choice of several trails. They can take the morning-sun-dappled West Way, a long cruise down the 1,140 ft. vertical drop that empties out into another lift-serviced area, where they have 2 choices: either straight on the open slopes or off to the left on the much steeper Ace of Spades trail. Or they can ski the Upper or Lower Glades to the S-curved Slingshot trail under the lift. A final choice is to follow the easy West Way to the more challenging Upper and Lower Fox trails, a combination that rates as one of the top runs in the Berkshires.

Expert skiers will probably prefer the double chair that begins in front of the lodge and from the summit provides access to the demanding Exhibition, Whitetail and Jericho trails. With their sustained and fairly steep pitches, all three are considered the most challenging in the Berkshires. Exhibition is the widest, but it is also the most exposed and therefore has the iffiest conditions in respect to ice and wind.

There are bail outs, however. Intermediates can leave the lift three quarters of the way up the mountain and ski the popular 360, one of the area's original trails that ends in front of the lodge. Or intermediates — and novice skiers, too — can go to the top, then ski the 2 mi.-long meandering Left Bank, a trail through the woods rather than down the face.

Sometime in the next 2 or 3 years, Jiminy plans to install a triple or quad mid-mountain chairlift. This will give the better skiers an area to themselves since the base of the lift will be up the mountain and away from the main lodge. Jiminy also beefed up its snowmaking in 1990 to service Whitetail. As a side benefit, that snowmaking should also remedy some of the snow and ice problems on the E. side of the Exhibition Trail.

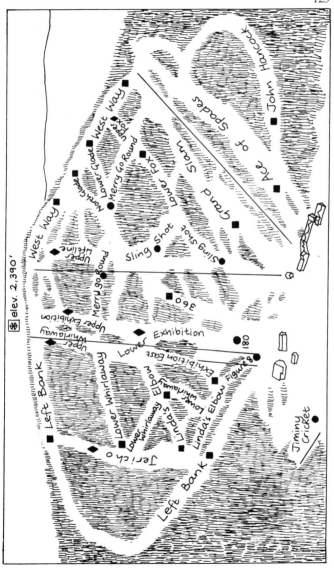

HANCOCK: JIMINY PEAK

Jiminy's summit offers one of the more spectacular Berkshire views, looking right up the Jericho Valley towards Vermont, with the Taconics on the left, the back side of Brodie Mtn. on the right. While not quite so wide open as the views from Catamount, Butternut or Bousquet, the vista gives a good feeling for the easy relationship between valleys and hills on the county's western border.

Other amenities are a nursery, a Ski-Wee program for tots and a state-of-the art rental equipment center where skis and boots are fitted in an assembly line process with separate entrances for incoming and outgoing skiers, to encourage an efficient traffic flow on busy days.

PERU

Peru is the highest town, in terms of elevation, in the county (and therefore the state), at 2,064 ft. It was incorporated July 4, 1771, as Partridgefield, because Oliver Partridge was one of the original purchasers of the grant. it began as a stop on a Boston to Albany stage line. The town was renamed in 1806, just two years after its western end had been lopped off to become Hinsdale, because like the country of Peru, it was in the mountains. And like the other Berkshire hilltowns, it subsisted on thin-soiled agriculture and a few mills, until young people heard of the kind of soil they grew out west. Then as now, residents went down to work in the more urban area of Pittsfield. With a population of under 750 and no shopping center, it remains one of the smallest Berkshire County towns. Few accommodations are available.

A 300-acre sanctuary near the center of town provides some excellent skiing.

CROSS COUNTRY

RICE SANCTUARY

Various trails available. Elevation: average above 2,000 ft.

Road approaches

Take Rte. 8 to Hinsdale; turn E on Rte. 143 to the center of town, recognizable because of the church on the left and the road junction. Turn right on South Rd. for .8 mi., then right again on Rice Rd. Park by the road. Ski up the drive.

DOROTHY FRANCES RICE SANCTUARY

The sign welcomes you to the Dorothy Frances Rice Sanctuary, and its visitors center, provided you arrive during daylight hours from May 28 to October 12. In the winter at Rice Sanctuary you're on your own, but local people also ski here.

Dorothy Frances Rice died of tuberculosis shortly after graduating from Smith College, in Northampton. She loved this site of the family summer home. After her father, architect Orville Rice of New York City, died, her mother, Mary Rice, set up a trust to maintain the 300-acre property named for her daughter. The family home partly burned and was partly chewed down by voracious porcupines.

People in Peru still talk about two Smith College girls who lived in the visitors' center for one or more summers while studying the plants and animals. Eventually the trust turned the property over to the New England Forestry Foundation, together with an endowment. NEFF, with headquarters in Boston, protects forest land and offers forest management services.

In warmer months, a caretaker comes for two days a week to maintain the trails and the building. Witness 72-year-old Mel Fassell of Pittsfield, who was caretaker of the property for a stretch of 25 years and provided most of this information.

The small building is the visitors' center. Nearby most of the trails come together, their arrows color coded, at a busy sign. Choose your color and follow in the direction of the arrow, because the trees are only "blazed," with colored blocks of wood, on one side. In other words, if you go the "wrong" way you won't see any blazes — although, for that matter, the trails are easy to follow. Choose your color and follow your trail.

You might want to follow the blue route, for example, which starts as a mowed section, zigs and zags through second-growth trees and weaves through stone walls, finally turning back on itself to return to the sign. For the most part, the trails, like this one, pass through old-field growth laced with stone walls. The length of the skis varies and, of course, it is possible to connect them in different ways as they cross each other. Figure on 30 min. to an hour — more if you want.

Yes, those are bear scratches on the shed, for the Peru wilderness is alive with fauna as well as flora. Although as many as 1,500 people wander through the sanctuary a year, you probably won't see any more of *them* than you do the bears.

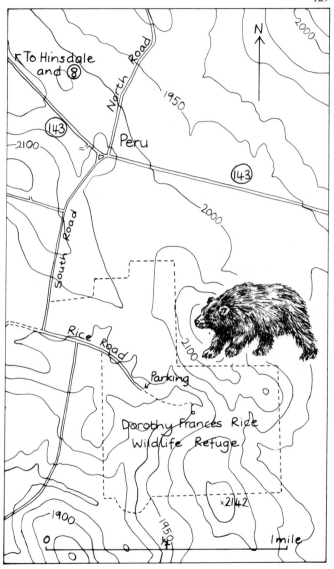

To Hinsdale
and ⑧

North Road

⟨143⟩

Peru

⟨143⟩

2100

1950

2000

South Road

Rice Road

Parking

2100

Dorothy Frances Rice
Wildlife Refuge

×2142

1900

1950

0   0   1 mile

0

N

2000

PERU: RICE SANCTUARY

WINDSOR

Once Plantation No. 4, the land making up Windsor was sold to a consortium of buyers in 1762, prototypes of today's land developers: buy a chunk of wilderness, survey it, and try to sell the lots for a good profit. The boundaries weren't exactly the same, including then part of present day Dalton and Cheshire but not the present northern part of Windsor — which was considered a section of plantation No. 5, Cummington (in Hampshire County).

As sometimes happens to developers even now, the lots moved slowly, which made it hard for the consortium to pay off its notes; furthermore, many of those who bought were also speculators rather than pioneers, so time passed before any significant settlement. Still, in 1771, residents petitioned to incorporate as Gageborough, after the pre-Revolutionary governor of the colony. In 1777 they petitioned to change the name, British Gen. Gage having fallen out of favor in 1776. By the end of that century, the area was a thriving farming community, with the usual accumulation of mills. When the sons and daughters of farmers went west and when the railroad failed to pass through town, Windsor became a byway.

By the beginning of the 20th century, Gen. Alfred E. Bates had begun accumulating former farms in the north of town, while Helen Gamwell Ely was accumulating land to the south to form her Helenscourt. In the 1920s, Elizabeth C.T. Miller bought the Bates estate. Mrs. Ely remarried Lt. Col. Arthur D. Budd, who also acquired the Miller property. Thus, the 3,000 acres of Notchview Reservation, nearly a quarter of the town, resulted from the union of two large estates, located on Rte. 9. Now owned by the TTOR, Notchview borders 1,616 acres of Windsor State Forest and is nearby a similar-sized tract that is part of the state forest and part of a wildlife management area, presumably fixing the character of the town for some time to come.

Camping

Although there is a nearby state park, Windsor Jambs, it is not available for winter camping, nor is Notchview open for camping. There are no tourist accommodations available in Windsor. Consult other town and trail descriptions.

CROSS COUNTRY

NOTCHVIEW

*5.1 miles of trails described here; 16 kilometers of groomed trails overall. Elevation: 2,000 to 2,160 ft. Novice to Intermediate. Donation. **684-0148***

Road approaches

Take Rte. 9 E. from Pittsfield through Dalton. The entrance to Notchview is 1.0 mi. E. of the junction with Rte. 8-A. That road, recently rebuilt after years of axle bending, drops S. from Rte. 116 out of Adams, an alternative course for people setting sail from North County.

NOTCHVIEW

You drive on an old section of Rte. 9 to the drive and parking lot that faces the Arthur D. Budd Visitors' Center, where you can use the facilities and wax your skis. You are asked to donate $5 per adult for the use of the property. The Trustees of Reservations maintains this 3,000-acre reservation, including grooming the ski trails. The place takes its name from the view from Lt. Col. Budd's former home, to the southeast, through a notch to the Cummington hills. Budd, a World War II hero, donated the property in 1965.

Snaking through the trees and mowed fields are 25 mi. of trails. The recommendation here is a route that varies from easy to intermediate, beginning at 2,000 ft. and rising 160 ft. The large map of the trails has a waxing thermometer attached for your convenience. Head N. from the map up and over the Ant Hill Loop for .6 mi. to left at an intersection on the Judges Hill Trail. All the signs you need are there. A short hop takes you to Shaw Rd., a broad snowmobile route and, in the right conditions a glorious run, down which you sail for almost 1.0 mi. to the Bumpus Trail, left, that takes you onto the fields that surrounded the Gen. Bates homestead. You could practice your telemark turns on Shaw Rd. or the Bates fields. If you come to the plowed section of Shaw Rd., you've gone too far.

Work up the fields to the Minor Trail, a wonderful, winding run across Bates Rd. and through evergreens to the highest point on this tour; and then down, across Shaw Rd. After crossing Shaw Brook on a bridge you have numerous choices to return to your car. The most direct is the Mixed Wood Trail, right, to the unnamed service road that parallels Rte. 9, NW to the Visitors Center. Again, the ample signs recommend the best route back.

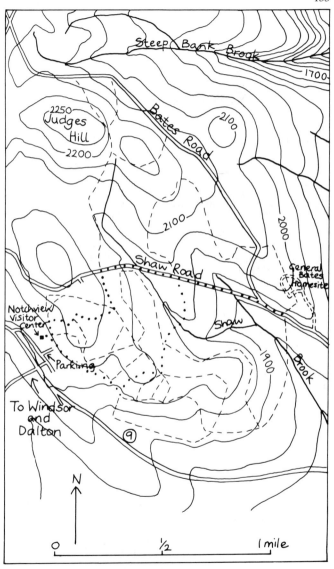

WINDSOR: NOTCHVIEW

NORTH COUNTY

CHESHIRE

Cheshire in early days was called New Providence by homesick Rhode Islanders. Col. Joab Stafford led a group of his townspeople to the Battle of Bennington on August 17, 1777. A monument and a wildlife management area honor him. In 1801 the town combined all its milk production for one day into a 1,255-pound cheese, pressed in a cider press, which oxen dragged to a boat on the Hudson River and thence to Washington to honor newly elected President Thomas Jefferson. Most of the Cheshire lakes, the headwaters of the Hoosic River, falling within the town borders, were dammed to provide a head at low water for the former Adams Print Works. The AT crosses the river and Rte. 8 in the center of town on its way to climb into the Mt. Greylock State Reservation via Outlook Ave. (The National Park Service is contemplating some changes in the route.) Many through-hikers on the trail stop in Cheshire to pick up mail forwarded to them c/o General Delivery at the post office and to sleep at a friendly church.

CROSS COUNTRY

HOOSIC RIVER RAILROAD

4.5 miles, Elevation: 934 to 890 ft.

Road approaches

This ski is best enjoyed by using 2 cars. Leave auto No. 1 on the dead end of a short street at the Rte. 8 overpass in the south end of Adams (the idea is to have the car on the same side of the river as the tracks). Park No. 2 at the Rte. 8 roadside rest beside the reservoir or at the rest-aurant across from it. You ski downstream.

HOOSIC RIVER RAILROAD

You need not worry about trains along this section of tracks, although hope springs eternal in the breasts of local railroad buffs that freight and scenic service will be re-stored . . . some day. In the mid-19th century the Hoosic River Railroad was an important artery. Now it is a wonderful, water-level route, along shiny parallel rails, primarily frequented by four-legged game and waterfowl.

Take off on the tracks at the nearby grade crossing, by the reservoir dam. Cross the bridge over Kitchen Brook. You pass by some back yards with barking dogs. Play the part of the train as you cross Church St., route of the AT as well as automobiles. Soon you are removed from houses and dogs, as South Brook enters from the SE. Stafford Hill rises NE and the Greylock massif, NW.

Natives call this section the Jungle, as the 10-ft. wide Hoosic writhes through swampland. The calcareous (lime-based) wetlands W. of the tracks, and marshes and shrub swamps E. of the tracks, are fine habitat for a variety of water creatures, some of which are active in winter. Wood duck platforms dot the wetlands, deer and muskrat tracks follow the stream. You may see snowshoe hare, pheasant, occasional fox, and some naturally reproducing brown trout as well as stocked trout. Note that although heading N., you are going downstream. Rte. 8 is close at hand, but not noticeable except for the distant sound of a truck down-shifting. You see a gouged hillside of gravel pits to the left.

A brick building belonging to the town of Adams introduces the first road for 3.0 mi. This is the pumping station for 2 artesian wells. Around the corner appears a bridge. Skis nicely bridge the space between the ties on this open trestle. A snowmobiler, on the other hand, can get his runners caught in the guard rails.

Welcome to Cheshire Harbor, said to be named because it harbored runaway slaves, a lovely spot with an old swimming hole, somewhat silted in. Now the river is on the left, with Rte. 8 just the other side. You can see the stonework of a mill sluiceway. Follow the railroad under Rte. 8, where you will run out of snow. Remove your skis; you should see your car on the other side.

In theory it would be possible to ski from Coltsville in Pittsfield to Ashland St., No. Adams, where the Hoosic River Railroad joins the live one, coming from the Hoosac Tunnel. (Do not ski near tracks in use.) But you won't find a better stretch anywhere than the one you've just completed.

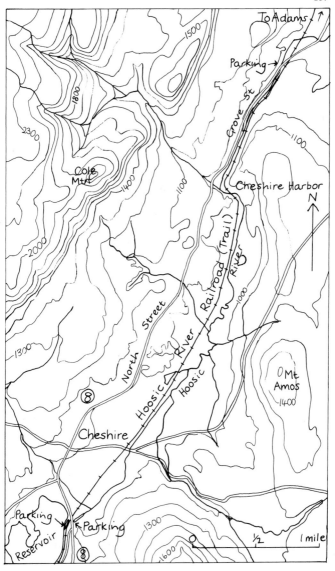

CHESHIRE: HOOSIC RIVER RAILROAD

NEW ASHFORD

According to tradition, pioneers building a stage road from Cheshire to Williamstown positioned a block house on the side of Greylock so they could see evidence of trouble ahead. Constructed out of lumber at hand in about 1750, it was the new ash fort that gave its name to New Ashford. The same road would have had to ford the Green River; maybe the two ideas became mixed together. The original settlers came from Rhode Island, Connecticut, and eastern Massachusetts, beginning in 1762. A marble quarry opened in 1822. A prosperous farming community in the 19th century, the town was incorporated in 1835. The state pushed through the Pittsfield-Williamstown Rd. (Rte. 7) in 1841. From 1916 to 1932, it was the first town in the country to record its vote in presidential elections, before New Hampshire towns got into the act. Now the home of the Kelly family's Brodie Mtn. ski area, it has 159 residents.

CROSS COUNTRY

BRODIE MOUNTAIN SKI TOURING CENTER

25 kilometers of groomed trails. Elevation: 1,400 to 1,700 ft. Fee. **443-4752**

Road approaches

Take Rte. 7 N. from Pittsfield or S. from Williamstown. Brodie is about midway. The ski touring center is on the E. side of Rte. 7, about 1 mi. S. of the parking lot for the downhill ski area. Parking is available here as well.

BRODIE MOUNTAIN SKI TOURING CENTER

The sign for this fine skiing center is off the road, on a drive that gives on to farm fields. A warming hut, with a flush toilet, is next to the parking area. The trails were laid out by

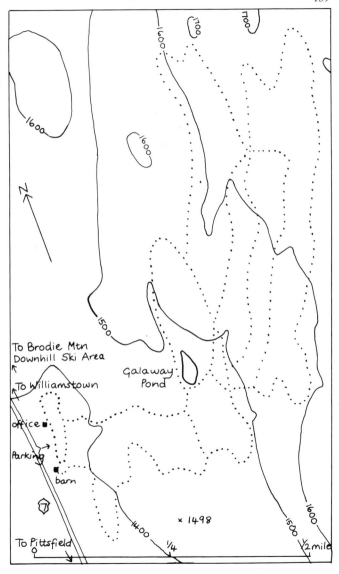

NEW ASHFORD: BRODIE MTN. SKI TOURING CENTER

Williams College Ski Coach Bud Fisher and are groomed by college employees, who are immortalized in trail names — at least those the college has applied. (The Kelly family, which owns Brodie, has added its Irish twist, in parentheses below.) The college nordic team trains and competes here.

Hoptoad (Killarney — well, it sounds Irish anyway) Field, at about 1,400 ft., next to the center, is a good place to learn to ski on a groomed and tracked loop. Tracks are often set running N, as well, over a cornfield. To get to the rest of the trails, follow the main trail up Andy's (Abby's) Climb to the (Gallaway) pond area, about 1,500 ft., where trails cross meadows and wooded land to the N. and S.

A sign guides you up to the next layer of trails, at about 1,600 ft.: Turkey Trot Lane, with good views, and Turkey Trot (Fleming's Lane) — which, if you follow S., has its own route down through Michie's (Mickey's) Meadow to the S. end of Hoptoad Field. Bud's Run Loop (Ring of Kerry) takes you up to 1,700 ft., at the top of the ridge, for the smoothest, rolling skiing of all.

Call for information or to arrange a guided tour on Mt. Greylock.

DOWNHILL

BRODIE MOUNTAIN

Trails: 25 slopes and trails (30% Novice, 50% Intermediate, 20% Expert). Summit elevation: 2,700 ft. Vertical drop: 1,250 ft. Lifts: 4 double chairs and 2 novice rope tows. Snowmaking: 95%. Ski School, Ski Shop, Rentals, Two cafeterias, Nursery, Night skiing. Snowboards allowed. Located just off Rte. 7, halfway between Pittsfield and Williamstown. **443-4752**

Brodie is a gentle mountain with a noisy reputation, reflecting the extrovert personality of its owners, the Kelly family who early on called their area "Kelly's Irish Alps."

Expert skiers will be hard put to ski an alpine, leg-pumping trail, although they will find some interesting short sections. More typical, however, are the miles of gently undulating trails, with above-average snow conditions — thanks to management's conviction that snow should be made and spread around in huge quantities.

Brodie is also known for its entertainment in the upstairs Blarney Room that season after season attracts a young crowd, whose members enjoy partying just as much, and sometimes more, than skiing.

The resort is almost immediately reassuring for the beginner. The double chair on the left as the skiers approach the base lodge from the parking lot goes up only 1,000 ft. and releases its passengers onto a broad slope with plenty of runout. A second double chair, almost immediately in front of the lodge, goes up 4,000 ft. and serves 3 principal trails: the 1-mi. intermediate Shamrock; the 1-mi. slightly tougher Kelly's Leap; and the 2-mi. novice Paddy's Promenade. All 3 trails are heavily used during the season since they are the closest to the main lodge. Well lighted and extensively groomed, they serve the needs of the largest variety of skiers. They are also typical of the rest of Brodie's trails: wide, with fairly even pitches, and plenty of reassurance for beginners and intermediates.

More demanding choices do exist. Skiers who stay to their right at the top of Shamrock can find their way to Mickie's Chute, which has a wide-open, steeply pitched bottom section. Another choice, the most enjoyable on the mountain, is the short, but fairly steep Kelly's Leap. And a third is to cross the top of Paddy's, then meet the intermediate JFK trail at its halfway point.

The other trails, about a half-dozen, are serviced by the 2 remaining double chairlifts over to the right as the skiers leave the main lodge. One of them is Dot's Lift, the longest and highest in Massachusetts. The trails from the summit are all novice and intermediate, ranging in length from 1 mi. to the 2.25-mi. Tipperary. The name is apt, since it circles the long way around the north side of the mountain, affording magnificent views of Mt. Greylock, the highest mountain in Massachusetts.

Irish festivity is very much part of the Brodie experience. The Blarney Room literally erupts with wild festivity on St. Patrick's, which at Brodie is celebrated for 9 days of partying, tube racing, clowning, bagpiping, singing and slush-jumping. But most of the time, it is just a good place to relax after skiing, a comfortable perch for conversation, music and refreshment against a backdrop of skiers gliding down the mountain, as seen all winter through the wall-size windows facing the trail or from the balcony on a warm, sunny afternoon in the spring. For those who prefer a slightly cozier, more intimate atmosphere, the lodge also has an Irish pub in its basement. Brodie also offers year-round campgrounds, an off-premises indoor tennis and racquetball club, and chalet and efficiency apartment rentals.

What a great place for beginners and intermediates and for the unattached to meet. Most trails are long and easy, and the views of Mt. Greylock are impressive. If the weather's too cold or the conditions questionable, the Blarney Room's Irish-style hospitality fills the void.

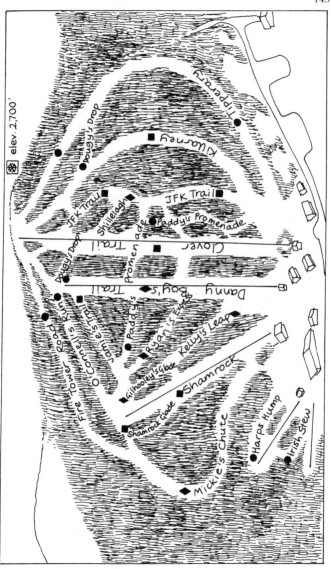

NEW ASHFORD: BRODIE MOUNTAIN

ADAMS AND MOUNT GREYLOCK

Adams, first East Township, then East Hoosuck, was finally named for Revolutionary War hero Samuel Adams in 1778. Its remarkable ethnic heritage began with English Quakers, whose vitality carved an industrial center from the wilderness, and continued through successive waves of immigrants who came to labor in those industries: Irish, Scots, German, French Canadians and Poles. Although the textile mills have ceased and although its northern end was lopped off to form No. Adams, Adams remains a bustling town of 10,000, with all the accommodations and services a skier could want. Most stores and restaurants are along Rte. 8, which goes by different names such as Columbia and Park streets. The statue of William McKinley in front of the library honors a friend of a foremost Adams family, the Plunketts. President McKinley's high tariff policies benefited the local cloth manufacturers.

Although the summit of Mt. Greylock lies in the town of Adams, the Mt. Greylock State Reservation encompasses 11,611 acres of hilly land in the towns of Adams, Cheshire, Lanesborough, New Ashford, No. Adams, and Williamstown. But you only have to look upwards in Adams to understand why the town feels a special regard for the mountain that looms over it. Mt. Greylock is a close, intimate friend.

Greylock is the tallest peak in southern New England at 3,491 feet. It is surrounded by half a dozen lower eminences, most of which are still higher than anything else in Massachusetts, Connecticut and Rhode Island: Saddleball (3,238), Mt. Fitch (3,110), Mt. Williams (2,951), Mt. Prospect (2,690), Stony Ledge (2,580), and Ragged Mtn. (2,451).

So it is not as high as some of the Adirondacks or the White Mtns. or the Green Mtns. even — which you can see from Greylock. At one time the Appalachians, of which Greylock is a part, stood Himalayan high, six times their present altitude, but time and weather have eroded them. Even in the early 19th century, before the more spectacular, western scenery in this country was accessible, Greylock created a lot of excitement.

All the great American writers and naturalists, like Thoreau, Hawthorne, and Melville, made their pilgrimages to Greylock. The first person to publish an account of his visit, in 1800, was the former president of Yale, Timothy Dwight, who said "the view was immense and of amazing grandeur. . ." It inspired prose, poetry, fiction and energetic enjoyment of the out-of-doors.

A popular destination as it has been and still is, not surprisingly, paved roads from No. Adams (Notch Rd.) and from Lanesborough (Rockwell Rd.) meet a mile from the summit, to which they travel together as Summit Rd. All are available to snowmobiles and skis in the winter. Greylock Rd. gravel-surfaced, climbs from the west to Rockwell Rd. not far below a gravel spur known as Sperry Rd. This provides a way to the public tentsites distributed discreetly in a spruce grove. Stony Ledge, at the end of Sperry Rd., provides a spectacular view of the Hopper, a V-shaped wedge worn by erosion on the western side.

The summit has limited development, such as broadcast towers and communications dishes. A 100-ft.-high War Memorial Tower, designed originally to be a lighthouse in the Charles River estuary, 130 miles away, was erected on Greylock in the 1930s to pick up the spirits of local residents during hard times. The state-owned Bascom Lodge, built by the CCC during the New Deal and run by the AMC, provides modest accommodations and good, hearty food in season (reservations required).

A 7.8-mi. segment of the 2,050-mi.-long AT transects the reservation from S. to N., a ribbon that hangs over most of the peaks. Remember: the AT is blazed white. Of the 7 three-sided shelters on the reservation, one is associated with the AT. Ten side trails to the AT, blazed blue — together with the roads, 11 other trails and the AT — total over 50 mi. of skiing in the Greylock range. The routes, shorter or longer, steeper or more gentle, fit just about every skier's time and ambition.

Most of the vegetation on Greylock is northern hardwood: beech, birch, maple and few evergreens. In the southern portions of the reservation, recent second growth fills formerly farmed fields. Here and there on the mountains' steep slopes stand aged trees, in areas not cut for railroads or other development over the years. Especially the 1,600 acres of the Hopper, on the west side contain red spruce stands nearly 200 years old. The state has designated the Hopper a Natural Area. The federal government, together with the Society of American Foresters, has recognized these spruces as a National Natural Landmark. To protect the Hopper, it is a low-impact area, excluding vehicles, campfires, and camping but available for study and skiing.

Its upper reaches are covered by a boreal type of balsam and yellow birch forest, probably the only example of such woods in Massachusetts. The bogs and stunted fir growth near the summits of Greylock and Saddleball are similar to the vegetation on the Canadian Shield — the fir forest of the far north. Your experience as a skier arriving in them is exhilarating.

Common wildlife include the whitetail deer, bobcat, snowshoe hare, cottontail rabbit, ruffed grouse, woodcock, raccoon, red squirrel, chipmunk, fox, skunk, woodchuck and the porcupine that hang around the shelters. Bear, the eastern coyote, wild turkey, fisher, and raven have recently returned to the reservation, as surrounding farm fields grow over.

Berkshire County is blessed by 150,000 acres of land protected from development, approximately one-quarter its total area. The Greylock Reservation stands as the flagship of the state's park system and as the jewel in the crown of the county public and private holdings.

Skiing on Greylock should be approached with caution, however. Heavy snow squalls can confuse even someone familiar with the terrain. A wind in exposed areas can convert a cold day to a frigid one. Do not attempt its steeper ascents and descents unless you are experienced and in good shape. Ski with others or, at least, leave word where you're going.

CROSS COUNTRY

ROCKWELL ROAD

6.5 miles of road, usually groomed. Elevation: 1,600 to 2,581 ft. Intermediate.

Road approaches

To get to the Visitors Center, turn E. on North Main St., N. of the town center on Rte. 7 in Lanesborough. Turn right on Quarry Rd. and bear left on Rockwell Rd., following the state reservation signs. Pass the administration building and garages on the left. From Rte. 7, it is 2.5 mi. to the stone-and-glass Visitors Center on the left.

ROCKWELL ROAD

This fairly gentle but lengthy ski begins at the Rockwell Rd. Visitors Center, zips along Rockwell Rd., which is unplowed in the reservation, circles up and over the nubbin called Rounds' Rock, and returns to the beginning. It is heavily used by snowmobilers but is wide, leaving room for skiers. A trail alternative exists for 1.0 mi. (This ski is not represented on the Mt. Greylock map, as it sticks largely to the road. Maps of the Brook and Berry Trail are available at the Visitors Center.)

The road route begins at the gate. If you want to try the Brook and Berry Trail (no snowmobiles) for the first part, leave the parking lot to the E., by the large map/sign. The trail begins as a nature trail, blazed orange, but follow straight by the stone wall, on blue blazes. As the trail approaches the brook, bear left on a trail blazed with red "xc" signs. This route avoids a brook crossing and steep section, but may not have been cleared recently.

It follows partway up a bowl W. and then E., .25 mi. until it crosses the brook and deposits you on the blue blazed trail again. Turn left. As you climb along the wall, right, the hemlock and mixed hardwoods give way to scrub growth.

You are entering the blueberry and blackberry part of the trail. It levels through scrub growth, gradually swinging W., away from the wall, until you come out on Rockwell Rd. (1.0 mi.).

A good outing? Turn left to return 1.0 mi. to the Visitors Center. Want to go twice as far again? Turn left to ski up the gently rising road to Rounds Rock. As the road begins to climb more steeply, after 2.0 mi., you come to a rocky hump, left, the beginning of the Rounds Rock Trail. Ski off the road and the hump to the trail opening; follow up the trail, through an open field, back into the woods, gradually swinging W., N., and E. back to the road above where you turned off. The Rounds Rock Trail runs .5 mi. Halfway around you pass the wooden remains of an airplane that crashed there while delivering New York papers to Berkshire in the 1950s. The 3.0 mi. return ski to the Visitors Center is glorious.

Even if you didn't make the ski, the view W. from the road to the Visitors Center and from its windows is worth the trip. The building, with facilities, is open year around, including weekends.

CROSS COUNTRY

BELLOWS PIPE / NOTCH ROAD

12.5 miles. Elevation: 1,304 to 3,941 ft. Expert.

Road approaches

Turn S. on Notch Rd., off Rte. 2 between Harriman-West Airport and the turn that leads to downtown No. Adams. The road climbs through a residential area and woods, turning sharply left at Mt. Williams Reservoir. After 2.4 mi. from Rte. 2, park along Notch Rd. before it turns right to enter the Mt. Greylock State Reservation; the road by Notch Reservoir comes in from the left. Do not park in such a way as to interfere with the private home at the corner. Bellows Pipe Trail is straight ahead.

Camping

You pass a lean-to, a ski shelter and Bascom Lodge on this ski. The lean-to is a bit more than halfway in time, where the Bellow's Pipe Ski Trail meets the Bellows Pipe (hiking) Trail. It faces south. The ski shelter, next to the parking lot at the summit, has a large fireplace in the middle and open sides; it is meant for day use but can provide some shelter for emergencies in the winter. Bascom Lodge, the AMC-run lodging in season, is closed in the winter. Two days a week the building beside the T.V. broadcast tower is open.

BELLOWS PIPE / NOTCH ROAD

You go up steeply by trail, and return more gradually on Notch Rd. Do not undertake this ski unless you feel fit. This is the most physically demanding tour in this book, but it is hard to think of a better place to be on a sunny day with light, powdery snow — on skis.

You are starting at 1,304 ft. in elevation and climbing to 3,491 in 4.0 mi. As you cross the chain on the road, it's clear you're on No. Adams watershed property, which protects Notch Reservoir, an impoundment of the brook that cuts the valley you climb. There are no blazes on city land, which extends to the Notch. The large sugar maples beside the gravel road have been there many generations; the pines were planted as a way of having trees beside a reservoir that would not fill the water with leaves. You pass several cellar holes and old walls you wouldn't have noticed if the foliage were out. The road was uncommonly well made: edged with stone, built with a crown, ditched on the sides. In places it appears to have been cobbled.

For this and many other man-made features of the route, credit Jeremiah Wilber and his descendants, who cut a spacious and productive farm out of the wilderness of this mountain about 1800, constructed the first road to the summit, grew hay, boiled off enormous quantities of maple syrup, grazed his cattle, killed marauding wolves and bears, built three mills and raised a dozen children by two wives.

Yours is the route Henry David Thoreau took in 1844 (not on skis, to be sure), when he heeded Hawthorne's and Emerson's advice to visit Greylock. (Emerson called it "a serious mountain.") At one of these homes, now a cellar hole, Thoreau stopped to converse with a lady who was combing her long tresses. You can read about it in *A Week on the Concord and Merrimack Rivers*. He spent the night on a wooden tower on the summit. When he awoke, the clouds had closed in below him, and he found himself, "in a country such as we might see in dreams, with all the delights of paradise."

In 10 min. you come to a yarding area used for timber cutting, but continue straight on the unblazed trail. The going gets a bit steeper. Soon, through breaks in the foliage, you can see the ridge of Ragged Mtn. (which rises 2,451 ft.), to the E., over Notch Brook valley. The next landmark is a bridge.

Having crossed a dozen or more tributaries, you finally cross the main stem of Notch Brook and, after a short, very steep eroded section, are in the Notch (2,197 ft. in elevation, 2.0 mi. from the start), clear not long ago as an orchard. An unmarked trail follows the wall up to the cliffs on Ragged. Now that you are on state land, look for orange and blue blazes that lead to the summit.

Follow a level section, looking down into Adams. Turn right on the blazed trail (the original road continues down to become Gould Rd. in Adams). The shelter is on your right, almost immediately. Take a blow. You are now on the Bellows Pipe Ski Trail, cut by the CCCs in the 1930s, as you will recognize from the series of steep, sharp switchbacks. After heading S., do not take the unmarked trail straight ahead, which leads to the Thunderbolt alpine ski trail. Instead, follow right, on a section that is a real workout.

The trees become lower and more scraggly on the steep eastern face — more beech and birch, somewhat stunted. After 5 switchbacks and testing ascents, you come out on the white-blazed AT, heading S. to the summit. Trees are often ice-covered on this stretch in the winter; if you catch them when the sun hits, the light sparkles off the crystals as though you were walking through a lighted chandelier. If a breeze is blowing, the branches clink together like cut glass, as well. Soon the AT joins the Thunderbolt Trail for the final assault. A blue-blazed trail heads right, crossing nearby Notch Rd. to Robinson's Point. You continue on the steep Thunderbolt to Summit Rd., which you follow right to the summit, 4.0 mi. of hard work from the start.

The summit may be blown clear, as may the road. After you have soaked up the views, while hidden from the wind behind the tower, and feel sufficiently rested, it is time to head down. Once or twice a winter someone will try to ski the Thunderbolt. It should not be you, as the trail has not been maintained since its glory days in the 1930s as the site of national downhill races. You are also advised against trying to ski down the way you came up. Rather, pass the entrance to the parking lot and follow the road, not too steep, with terrific views over the edge, especially into the Hopper. At the junction, bear right to No. Adams. The total road trip is more than 8.0 mi. In the middle section you may have to stride or skate; but it keeps going down. Deceptively, towards the bottom, about when your knees are getting wobbly, it gets steeper and curvier, so that by the time you must avoid a gate at the bottom, you may have to take a dive. A hundred yards below the gate you come out at your car.

CROSS COUNTRY

CHESHIRE HARBOR

12 miles. Elevation: 1,800 to 3,100 ft. Expert.

Road approaches

At the statue of former President McKinley in front of the library in Adams turn W. off Rte. 8 onto Maple St. At .4 mi. turn left on West Rd.; .5 mi. later, right on W. Mountain Rd. at sign for Mt. Greylock Greenhouses. The road ends at a turn-around, the site of a former farmhouse, after 1.6 mi.

Camping

Peck's Brook shelter, a three-sided, Adirondack lean-to, is attained by a separate, 1.25-mi. trail that departs from the junction of Rockwell, Notch and Summit roads. All summit buildings are closed from late October until Memorial Day, but some protection can be found at the Thunderbolt Ski Shelter, an open-sided shelter with a fireplace on the AT just below the summit parking lot, to the north of the War Memorial Tower, or two days a week in the building beside the T.V. broadcast tower.

CHESHIRE HARBOR

Mt. Greylock is very close to its east side approaches, although the summit is more of a haul than it looks as you stand on the old field at the end of the open section of West Mtn. Rd. The route described does not go to the summit, although to do so would only add 2.0 mi. of relatively easy going. Cheshire Harbor Trail rises from 1,800 to 3,491 ft. It is heavily traveled by snowmobiles, packing the surface to ice at times. The entire trail starts at a community in Cheshire (Cheshire Harbor) about 1 mi. W. of where you start, apparently named because it harbored runaway slaves before the Civil War.

The unblazed trail leaves as a woods road, heading from the SW corner of the field. Old walls mark the site. Almost immediately the portion of the trail rising from Cheshire Harbor enters left.

After the sweat starts flowing you come to the first switchback and, in 3 more min., to the second, where a trail enters left (ignore it). Soon you see the summit, with its tower, rising over Peck's Brook ravine. After a mi. you round the third switchback and, soon, the junction with Old Adams Rd. makes the fourth. You will return here on the way back.

You bear right, staying on the Cheshire Harbor Trail, however, continuing up the moderate grade that characterizes this entire trail. The trail has been blazed blue or orange from time to time, although blazes are not needed. The northern hardwoods through which you pass are severely stressed, the effect of atmospheric pollution. Scientists have designated plots in the area to study the decline of high altitude forests in New England. The results to date are disturbing. You see many dead birch, beech, and maple. The ledges (left) rise to the ridge that connects Greylock with the next peak S., Saddleball.

After you cross Peck's Brook, a snowmobile trail, known as the Super Highway, drops right to the Gould Farm. Continue on to Rockwell Rd., 3.0 mi. from the car. To get to the summit, turn right and then bear right at the junction.

Turn left for what in proper conditions is a delightful 3.5 mi. downhill ski with excellent views of the valleys of New Ashford and Brodie Mtn. You pass Sperry and Greylock roads, on the right, and then the open area, left, where blueberry pickers park in the summer. There are no signs but a well-defined trail passes through the only cleared land on that side. You are passing just below the end of the Saddleball ridge, known as Jones' Nose, for a 19th-century farmer who had a farm there. Then begins a steep downhill you may wish to walk. Snowmobile traffic, again, may have left the trail glazed.

The old AT route exits right, across the stream at the bottom of the hill. Old Adams Rd., which you are now on, runs without any more long steep sections, swinging N. where the new AT crosses. Immediately after that the private Red Gate Trail exits right. This is also a delightful rolling section, interrupted occasionally by abrupt dips for stream crossings. The entire Old Adams Rd. section back to Cheshire Harbor Trail extends 3.0 mi. You swing around a sharp corner to discover you need to make an even more abrupt right to head downhill to your car. Again, due to traffic, this section may require walking.

CROSS COUNTRY

ROARING BROOK / STONY LEDGE

9.0 miles . Elevation: 1,100 to 2,500 ft. Expert.

Camping

You are skiing to Sperry Rd. Campground, spacious always but certainly not crowded in the winter. You pass a three-sided lean-to at the top of Stony Ledge Trail.

Road approaches

Beginning at Field Park in Williamstown, drive S. on Rte. 7, 5.5 mi. to Roaring Brook Rd., left just before the Massachusetts Department of Public Works garage; alternately, coming from the S., after entering Williamstown, turn right immediately beyond the garage. Drive 1 mi. up the gravel road until you see the sign indicating the private Mt. Greylock Ski Club. Use the parking area large enough for 3 or 4 cars just downstream from the sign; in the unlikely event that area is filled, you will have pull over nearer Rte. 7.

ROARING BROOK / STONY LEDGE

This tour requires more skill than any other in this book, especially on the steep descent. You can call the loop Stony Ledge for the high point with its spectacular view of the Hopper, but you actually ski up the Roaring Brook Trail. You rise from a deep valley through a hemlock forest, along the plateau that hosts a campground and down a mixed hardwood trail. The route described does not go to the summit, a sidetrip that would add 5.0 mi.

The trailhead is streamside, across from the ski club sign. You begin on a well-established old woods road, blazed blue for the most part, although some of the previous white blazes persist. In 3 min. you hope to cross Roaring Brook on ice. If that's not possible, crawl across a convenient tree that bridges the brook. You climb, passing a trail that rises into the fields, left. You drop down to the brook again and cross it on a log bridge. Next you cross a plank bridge.

The sign indicates the wide, Stony Ledge Trail to the left to be an "intermediate ski trail," which refers to downhill skiing. Since you will descend that way, it will interest you to know that nordic skiers should be advanced to use it. Although you can see how the CCCs laid it out wide enough to enable some maneuvering, it hasn't been maintained for skiing for years in spite of the sign.

Go straight, rather than up Stony Ledge, even though that means crossing a brook, and then climbing beside it. Climb steadily, following white blazes, with steep brook valleys on either side until, about 1.5 mi. from beginning, the trail begins to level. The Deer Hill Trail enters right. You cross a bridge over Roaring Brook, follow on its south side, then cross another bridge. From the end of that follow the road to Sperry Rd. If you turn right, you could ski to Rockwell Rd. and the summit, Old Adams Rd. (see Cheshire Harbor Trail), or the Visitors Center (see Rockwell Rd. ski).

Turn left (N.) for a pleasant, gently rising ski for 1.0 mi. to Stony Ledge. Stop. Look over the Hopper to the mass of Greylock. Inured to spectacle as you may be, this sight will exhilarate. On the wall opposite you can see dark stands of red spruce, some nearly 200 years old, probably the oldest stands in the Commonwealth. You can also see March Cataract, to the SE, as a ribbon of ice.

To begin the return to your start, turn 180 degrees away from the view (right angles to the way you came), pass the corner of the shelter, and shortly you will be at the head of the Stony Ledge Trail. It gets steeper. An additional complication, unless it is quite cold, is a lot of water, some of which meanders in the trail. There are also rocks. You've been warned. On the other hand, with heavy powder — remembering that applying the body to the side of the slope slows the descent — it can be negotiated.

So, go to it. There is room to maneuver, which doesn't exist on the Roaring Brook Trail. After 4 or 5 sharp dips, the descent slows and remains good xc going until it merges with Roaring Brook Trail, at Roaring Brook. Follow back the way you began. Cross the brook twice on bridges, once by improvisation, and then you'll be at the Roaring Brook Rd., a few hundred ft. from your automobile.

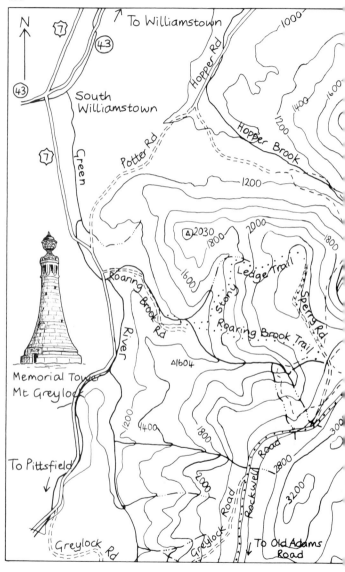

ADAMS: MT. GREYLOCK

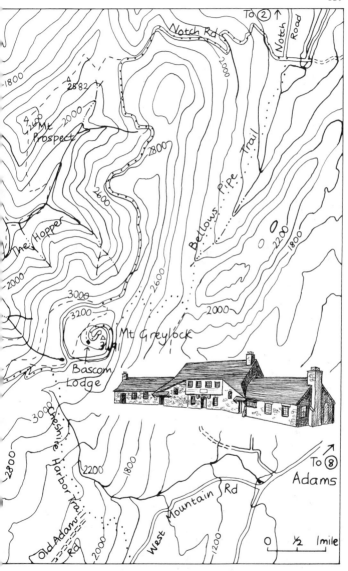

To ② ↑

Notch Rd

Notch Road

1800

△ 2582

Mt Prospect

2000

2800

Bellows Pipe Trail

The Hopper

2600

2000

0

2200

1800

3000

3200

2000

Mt Greylock

Bascom Lodge

3000

2800

Cheshire Harbor Trail

2200

1800

To ⑧ ↑ Adams

West Mountain Rd

1200

Old Adams Rd

2000

0   ½   1mile

ADAMS: MT. GREYLOCK

WILLIAMSTOWN

Soldiers at Fort Massachusetts, once located where the Price Chopper supermarket now resides on Rte. 2 in No. Adams, built the first homes in the township west of the fort and held their first Proprietors' Meeting there in 1753. Then a flare-up of the French and Indian War drove them out; of the original residents only Benjamin Simonds returned, with a wife, after having been in prison in Quebec. Their daughter, Rachael, was the first child of European stock born in the area. Simonds' River Bend Tavern still stands, run now as a bed and breakfast, on Simonds' Rd. (Rte. 7 north of town).

Still an active farming town, Williamstown is more famous for the college that has grown up with it. Ephraim Williams, Jr. was a commander at the fort; on his way to battle at Lake George in 1755, he rewrote his will to establish a secondary school for the children of his command. Town and school were named for his generosity. The trustees converted his school into Williams College, which opened in 1793.

The college has attracted to the community the Clark Art Institute, with its ravishing collections of French Impressionists and 19th-century American artists and sculptors, and the Williamstown Theatre Festival, busy all summer with myriad main stage and experimental productions, readings and cabarets. Both have been singled out by tough critics as the best of their kind in the United States. Just as the college's art museum complements the Clark, other professional and amateur theater and music groups complement the WTF. Yet it is the town's natural landscape you will read about in this volume.

Should the weather turn sour, however, despair not. The Clark (open daily except Monday) provides an eyeful that can last all day. Other undercover destinations: the Williams College Museum of Art, the Hopkins Forest Farm Museum, the Chapin Rare Books Library, and the planetarium show at the Old Hopkins Observatory (reservations required). As well as shopping on Spring and Water streets, visitors may take tours of the Williams College campus, which originate at the admissions office, Main St.

CROSS COUNTRY

STONE HILL

Up to 4 miles. Elevation: 750 to 1,000 ft. Intermediate.

Road approach

For Williamstown's favorite ski route, drive S. on South St., beginning at Field Park, across from the Williams Inn. At a half mi., turn right into the Clark Art Institute. Drive under the bridge and turn left for the far side of the parking lot, behind the dark-colored main building.

STONE HILL

This ski, steep at the beginning, will take you from the Clark parking lot, 750 ft. in elevation, up the open hillside — with a striking view of downtown Williamstown, the Clark, the college, the Dome in southern Vermont, East Mtn. (encompassing Pine Cobble and Eph's Lookout), the Hoosac Valley heading into No. Adams, the Hoosac Range beyond the city, and the Greylock range — to a stone seat at 1,000-ft.; then along the former Stone Hill Rd. with a possible loop across private property. Although the several public and private landowners are cooperative, this unofficial route is not blazed.

Sterling and Francine Clark built the white marble building for their art collection. It was opened to the public in 1955. The darker building to the right was built as an addition to the institute in 1973. Head W. from the parking lot, through a ditch and gate in the fence above it. Bear left to an opening in the hedgerow that marks the bottom of the hillside. Head directly up the hill to the group of trees at the ridgeline. (Many prefer to make the loop clockwise, to finish on this hillside. The advantage of the counterclockwise approach is that after the steep climb, the remainder is a long, gradual downhill.)

Drop down the backside of the ridge. A cart track crosses the field S. to the woods. Follow it. Once in the woods, the trail swings left and rises to the remains of the Colonial Stone Hill Rd., which preceded Rte. 7 as the main N.-S. route in the county, at the stone seat erected as a memorial to George Moritz Wahl. He was a professor of German at Williams College, who was incorrectly suspected by some of being a German spy during World War I. He was accustomed to climbing to this spot in the evening to watch the sunset — in those days the view was treeless. This monument was the town's posthumous apology and tribute.

Having passed through the gate, continue S. on the old road, to see how the hill got its name. If you look through the trees to your left, you will see the schist outcroppings. A stone hill, all right. The road passes through woods, losing elevation, and then begins to climb. There is an open field on your right. Near the crest, a trail goes off left, beside a cornfield. It follows down slightly to an open gate, the invitation of the kind landowner. You are halfway (2.0 mi.). For a 2-car variation on this route, you could stay on Stone Hill Rd. another .5 mi. to the end of the plowed section, in from Scott Hill Rd.

Beyond the gate the trail has been rerouted because of a blow-down, but in general you bear right (S.) again and then left on another old road. There is a pond on your left, but you probably won't notice it. As you follow along, a new view of the Hopper on Greylock, with the mansion at Mt. Hope, swings into view. The road crests a small outcropping, where it's likely to be blown clear of snow, then passes through another gate, more woods, and swings down, bearing right, with another good view of Greylock. The road continues through another gate and across the field beyond, but you want to bear left (N.) at this point, aiming for a break in the tree line that borders that field.

Crossing through the trees, you are on another field, belonging to Williams College, where a NW wind may be quite cold. Swing generally left again, rising to a knoll where

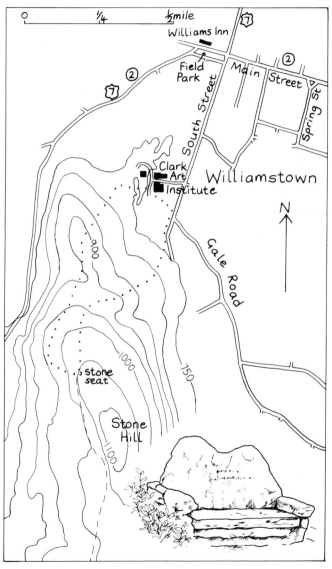

WILLIAMSTOWN: STONE HILL

you are faced with the buildings of High Croft School on your right and a sloping field, left. Traverse the field, past the school buildings, until you come out on Gale Rd., straight ahead. (If snow and wind conditions are just right, you may be able to follow tracks, left, at the bottom of the hill, that cross a small brook and Buxton School land back to South St. just S. of the Clark, but the route is difficult to describe.)

For an easier to describe route, ski beside or walk down Gale Rd. to the golf course on the right. Follow along the fence to an open gate, then ski the golf course, bearing left to a point across South St. from the Clark. You left your car behind the Clark. If no golf course gate is open, simply stay on Gale Rd., which becomes South St. at the Buxton School corner.

CROSS COUNTRY

RRR BROOKS

7.75 miles, plus 2 miles. Elevation: 800 to 2,200 ft. Expert.

Camping

The Williams Outing Club cabin in Hopkins Forest is available through the club to people associated with Williams College. No other shelters or camping are available on this route. Hopkins Forest, a 2,500-acre tract bordering New York and Vermont, is an ecology laboratory for Williams College. Please do not wander off the trails because you might inadvertently disturb experiments. Signs explain some of the work in progress, much of which currently has to do with monitoring the effects of acid rain on trees. As alternatives to this route, see the following section on ski trails in Hopkins Forest. Pocket maps are available at the large map near the barn.

Road approaches

From Field Park in Williamstown drive W on Main St., down and up, to a left turn on Northwest Hill Rd. Turn right for .5 mi., past the head of Bulkley St. Turn left into the Hopkins Forest parking lot. If you have a second car, drive back the way you came about 1.5 mi., turning right off Main on Thornliebank and right again on Rtes. 7 & 2. Park on the shoulder if there is room, at the foot of Bee Hill Rd. If there's no room, you may be able to park along Thornliebank.

RRR BROOKS

Although this ski is called the Triple-R Brooks Trail, actually it travels 5 trails. A vigorous outing, you climb from 800 ft. to 2,200 ft. As well as evidence of past land use, you view two spectacular brook valleys and, standing

200 ft. above the highway, an eagle's-eye look at the old Petersburg Pass ski area, Berlin Mtn., the Hopper on Greylock, and the Williamstown valley. Remember that cold comes with altitude and that the Taconic Ridge can be extremely windy. On the other hand, standing on the top of this piece of the world in snow and ice crystals is unforgettable. The three states, Williams College, and Williamstown are cooperating to create a public recreation area for 3,500 acres in this area.

Beginning at the Hopkins Forest lot, ski up the private drive to the barn. Turn right, past the WOC cabin and the maple sugar house. Continue on this woods road, well made by the CCC when the U.S. Forestry Service ran an experimental forest here. Pass without entering a weather station (4 min.) that gathers important information for experiments in the forest. Looking down to your right, you will soon see Ford Glen, in the chasm it has cut for itself.

You are on what is known as the Loop Trail. Bear right at the first intersection (1.0 mi.) and straight at the second. You gradually gain elevation through second-growth birch and maple — all this land was open fields two generations ago. Bear left where a private road enters right. Just before the brook crossing, turn right on the Birch Brook Trail (2.0 mi.).

After the broad, gently sloped Loop Trail, rocky and steep Birch Brook Trail is a shock; nevertheless, follow by the brook for a few hundred yards. Then turn right, up the side of a shoulder. This trail soon parallels the remains of a stone wall and swings left on top of the rise. Another wall and forest boundary appear right. The large maples here were never cut because they were (and are) line trees, marking a property boundary.

Cross a spring, beginning a steep, steady ascent to the ridge on the left. The forest here is older, although the birches and maples are not healthy. Climbing over phyllite outcrops, after watching your elevation approach the ridge's for some time, at last, 3.5 mi. from the lot, you attain the Taconic Crest Trail (TCT), blazed white. Make a hard left at the yellow sign. Snowmobiles are not allowed, although one may have been by.

Continue S. on the TCT, through mostly scrubby vegetation. You may want to add another layer of clothing, now that you've finished climbing and are at the mercy of the wind. Yellow signs and blue blazes, .9 mi. from cresting the crest, warn of the Shepherd's Well Trail. Turn left on a much less used trail. You will soon confirm you're on the trail by seeing Hopkins Forest postings to your left. Work up the sidehill. Where the trail may appear to go straight through a clearing, it actually angles left along a ridge. Soon you break out into steep-sloping blueberry bushes, high over the highway (Rte. 2), facing the old Petersburg Pass ski area, now owned by the New York State Department of Environmental Conservation. As you work your way around a shoulder, carefully — especially if at all icy — you see Berlin Mtn., with the telltale streak of the old Williams College ski trail, and the fields rising to the Hopper on Mt. Greylock. Winter wind and heavy snow can obscure the trail, which soon returns into the woods.

You work down at first gradually and then steeply, coming out on an old cut, where trees were once removed to let wires through, at about 4.0 mi. Turn left, downhill, with views of the Congregational Church spire and college chapel tower lined up. Turn right on a wide and grassy logging road, which soon joins the Triple-R Trail. Dean of the College RRR Brooks built a log home you will see across the pond at the foot of this trail and laid out the trail, largely on existing old roads. For example, the trail here appears to be on Petersburg Rd. before the lower Taconic Trail State Highway was built in the 1930s. Brooks dug the lowest part of the trail out of the sidehill, with pick and shovel.

For a way, you follow a wall, left. After .7 mi. on the woods road, jog left, swing right, and cross old Petersburg Rd. (you may be whizzing) to come out on an old farm field the state mows occasionally, part of Taconic Trail State Forest. The run across this field can be exciting; tuck. Follow the tracks to the corner farthest down. The clump of trees to the left marks a cellar hole.

Back in the woods, follow a shoulder between 2 rivulets, across a bridge at a boggy area. Flora Glen, which you keep on the left for the rest of this hike, is named not for a person but for plants. Dropping moderately, in 10 min. you round a steep, sharp corner, right, with a second bridge at the bottom. Some Brooks Trail skiers have frozen permanently into the snowplow position at this point. Soon you enter a lovely hemlock forest. The trees find it difficult to cling to the steep valley walls, as storms hurl them, roots and all, into the valley. Western Massachusetts' foremost early poet, William Cullen Bryant, may have been inspired by the wild romanticism of Flora Glen to write his "Thanatopsis" — in any case he liked the place. Eventually the trail drops right into the streambed, where the going can be wet and difficult. Then it climbs somewhat up the valley walls, on a narrow ledge. After 1.5 mi. from the edge of the field you arrive at a dam, beside Bee Hill Rd.: the end of skiing. Walk down the road 100 yards to Rtes. 7 & 2.

For an alternate route that allows the car to do most of the climbing, see the description of the Snow Hole ski.

CROSS COUNTRY

HOPKINS FOREST

Various trails available. Elevation: 801 to 1,300 ft.

Road approaches

To reach the parking lot, drive W. from Field Park to a right on Northwest Hill Rd. Continue .5 mi., past Bulkley St., to Hopkins Forest on the left. An alternative route: from Field Park drive N. on Rte. 7 to Bulkley St. Turn left, climb the hill, turn right on Northwest Hill Rd. and then almost immediately left at the forest entrance.

Camping

No camping, although a cabin is available by reservation to those associated with Williams College.

HOPKINS FOREST

Williams College owns this 2,500-acre former federal experimental forest, using it as a laboratory for ecology studies and as a conservation and recreation holding. Trails are available for skiing at no charge; trails are not groomed, nor does the college maintain facilities to benefit skiers. No motor vehicles are allowed on the trails; nor should you drive to the residence, up the drive.

The basic trail system is a figure-8, with a separate route to Northwest Hill Rd. to the left and another, up Birch Brook Trail to the Taconic Crest Trail (see the description of the RRR Brooks Trail). Most users ski right of the Moon Barn — having come up the drive from the parking lot — after studying the map on the sign there. This is a broad road, sometimes tracked but more often marked by a variety of skiers, walkers, dogs, and horses. After rising gently for 1.0 mi., you reach a 4 corners. For a 4.5 mi. spin, go straight or right to complete the larger loop, which has steep sections. Some skiers (perhaps unreconstructed downhillers), take a sharp left, in order to finish a steep downhill with a flourish beside the Moon Barn. Others are content to turn around and head back down the road (about 2.0 mi.).

Those who want to make the long loop might consider the ramifications of their choice at the corners. If you go right, you will rise gently, ski through another trail junction, cross a stream on a bridge, climb steeply, have a short level ski at 1,300 ft., cross a brook without a bridge, then start down steeply. At the bottom of the hill, you come to a steep right turn with a narrow bridge at the bottom. In other words, going counterclockwise in some conditions requires control at near expert level. Then you climb a gentle hill to the trail junction.

Alternately, choosing to start straight ahead at the junction begins you on a downhill, followed by a gentle rise. Cross the bridge and climb steeply beyond, which though strenuous, puts less strain on your ability to hit that bridge at high speed. This clockwise route leaves you with a fine downhill from the 1,300-foot plateau. At the first, steeper part, be alert for an eroded stretch of trail that has been corduroyed, i.e. filled with small logs, sometimes treacherous. The turns that follow are testing but, unless icy, doable by intermediate-level skiers, as is stopping at the brook crossing at the bottom. Ignore the private trail from the N. while you swing right.

Follow straight at the first junction. At the second, you have a choice of returning by the road or by the steep hill by the barn.

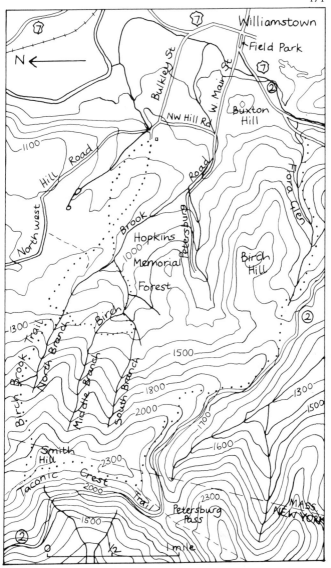

WILLIAMSTOWN: RRR BROOKS / HOPKINS FOREST

CROSS COUNTRY

FIELD FARM

2.8 mi. Elevation: 1,000 ft. Moonlight skiing. Novice.
*Donation. **458-3144***

Road approaches

From Field Park (named for a different Field, Cyrus W., who laid the Atlantic cable), drive S. on Rtes. 7 & 2. At the Five Corners, where Rte. 43 crosses, turn right and then right immediately on Oblong Rd. Follow this road as it rises to 1,000 ft., about one mi., to the Trustees of Reservations sign at the driveway to Field Farm. Turn right and bear right to the garage, the winter parking area.

FIELD FARM

The Trustees of Reservations own a 254-acre parcel at the foot of the Taconic Range, known as Field Farm after the farming family of Nathan Field, who worked the land for many years. Much of the land is indeed open field, which serves to characterize the skiing at this place, with some wooded land at the northern end and in the vicinity of the pond. The site is rich in wildlife, birds, and views. The route described here is level, with a slight up and down in the NW corner. The Trustees, who occasionally organize a moonlight ski, ask for a small donation for use of the area.

The property was donated in 1984 by Lawrence H. and Eleanore Bloedel. House and guest house, known as the Folly, were designed by Edward Goodell and Ulrich Franzen, respectively. Some of the outdoor statuary the Bloedels collected remains in place. The house is operated as a bed and breakfast by the Trustees, and reservations may be made through the telephone number listed above.

Ski N. from the garage, leaving the house to your left. Soon you will pick up the well-marked North Trail, which

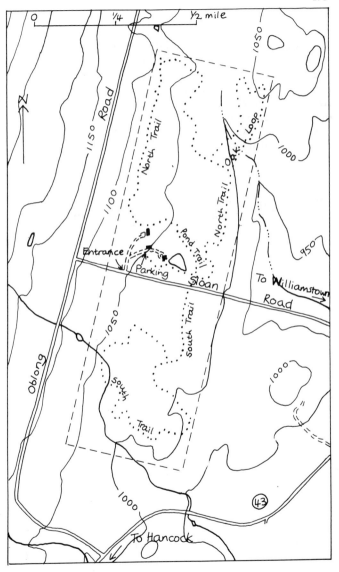

WILLIAMSTOWN: FIELD FARM

follows the property line. The land begins to rise as you pass through a fence, followed by a fairly steep although brief dip and sharp corner. You head E. and then swing S., before turning N. again on the Oak Loop, crossing the same fence twice. Back on the North Trail again, you pass through an orchard, pasture, fence and cornfield with a view W. You turn towards the house, then sharply away, through woods. Turn right, veer left alongside the pond. Shortly you will be back at the garage.

You may decide to do it again or to take the South Trail, from the W. end of the pond and across Oblong Rd., a 2.0-mi. spin. Moonlight skiing in general is wonderful, even though the indirection of the illumination leaves some surprises. This level area is especially good at night, not to mention the hot chocolate served after the organized moonlight skis.

DOWNHILL / CROSS COUNTRY

MOUNT GREYLOCK SKI CLUB

*Downhill trails: 4 Novice, 9 Intermediate, 3 Expert. Summit elevation: 1,700 ft. Vertical drop: 500 ft. Lifts: 2 rope tows. Lodge, outhouses. Groomed cross country trails. Cooperative club.**458-3060***

Road approaches

To get to Goodell Hollow, drive S. from Field Park on Rtes. 7 & 2. Stay on Rte. 7 where the roads divide. Just before the state Department of Public Works garage, S. of south Williamstown, turn left on Roaring Brook Rd. These are the same instructions as for the Stony Ledge ski, except continue up this narrow road at the ski club sign, as long as it is before 2 p.m. After 2 p.m., the road is one-way down. You must park at the bottom and walk up the .5 mi. People used routinely to strap on chains at the bottom of the road, which is not for the fainthearted. It has been improved in recent years, however, and is generally passable with snowtreads. Otherwise, well, the walk up is pleasant.

MOUNT GREYLOCK SKI CLUB

Did you bring your tow grips?

What?

Tow grips are metal handles to help hold on to a rope tow. They sound antique by the recent standards of skiing, but they work quite well at Goodell Hollow, where volunteers crank up the 1948 Ford and 1956 GMC engines on subzero mornings to start the rope whistling through the pulleys, drive the snow cat to groom the slopes, cut brush off the trails in the fall, and arrange social events year around.

A family-oriented, cooperative ski area, the purpose of the club has remained the same for fifty years: "To promote safe recreational and competitive skiing, to develop and improve the skiing technique of its members, to promote other outdoor activities throughout the year, and to encourage good fellowship among skiers."

Mount Greylock Ski Club is designed primarily to serve downhill skiers, but in recent years it has made an effort to accommodate cross country skiers as well. At least one of the downhill trails is negotiable on the long skis; in fact, those interested in telemark skiing would find this the perfect situation. As well, about 1.5 mi. of xc tracks are laid in the rolling fields at the base of the slopes. The Roaring Brook and Stony Ledge trails on Mt. Greylock are nearby. As far as that goes, it is possible for someone who knows his way to ski from Goodell Hollow, up Potter Rd., through Mt. Hope and over Stone Hill to the center of town, 6.0 mi. as the crow goes, only crossing 2 plowed roads.

Take a lunch. Drink the spring water. Eat in the lodge, heated by two woodstoves; or, if it's sunny, move a table outside in front of the lodge. Enjoy the fact that everyone looks out for everyone else — and their children. It is hard to imagine a better place to learn how to ski.

Without snowmaking, the ski area relies on nature and careful grooming. Since it faces N and the base is at 1,200 ft., however, it holds snow. The lifts run weekends and holidays, although cross country members are welcome any time. The club started in 1933, when a group of Pittsfield businessmen got together to promote skiing in Berkshire County. At that time in the United States, only a few half-crazies skied a few fringe places like Vermont and New Hampshire.

The same group assisted the CCC in cutting the famous Thunderbolt Ski Trail, on the E. side of Mt. Greylock, and helped Clarence Bousquet start his area in Pittsfield. They laid out the ski trails in the Pittsfield State Forest. Meanwhile they looked about for some land on which to start an area of their own, purchasing the present farm in 1937. As well as the farmhouse, where the caretaker lives, the club owns the ski lodge with do-it-yourself canteen, a spring, and men's and women's outhouses. The longest rope tow in the state, 1,350 ft., hauls skiers 400 ft. up, for a respectable vertical drop.

177

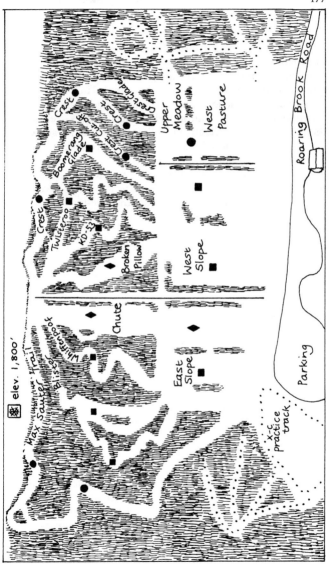

WILLIAMSTOWN: MT. GREYLOCK SKI CLUB

The abandoned lift served as a jump for the Williams College ski team from 1951 through 1960. The smaller rope tow serves a novice glade. The dozen downhill trails vary from quite easy to tough intermediate. The xc tracks in the field are a good place to practice your glide or skating; and to vary the regimen for families with mixed skiing interests. Yes, and there are sledding and toboggan hills for youngsters for whom enough skiing is enough on a given day. The club is home to a racing team of older youngsters.

If you would like to visit the area as a guest, call the number above.

Where else can you get a family membership for under $100?

NORTH ADAMS

North Adams was formed from Adams' rib in 1878, as an immediate result of the railroad coming through the Hoosac Tunnel into the north part of town — which then outstripped the south part. The incision was already there, though, created by a military line for recruiting soldiers for the Revolutionary War, and based on topography. The Hoosic River floodplains of the southern part lent themselves more to agriculture; the swift falling streams of the north part more to industry.

The slack in employment when the textile mills moved to the southern United States was taken up by the electronics industry, especially during World War II. But after the war, electronics, too, gradually faded. More recently, in the 1980s, the state has tried to help. It created Western Gateway Heritage State Park, an effort to revitalize the downtown by building a memorial to the railroad past and a home for shops and restaurants. The state purchased Natural Bridge, a marble span carved by a stream, from private interests. And the state is working with Williams College and other private groups to develop the largest museum of contemporary art in the world, Massachusetts MoCA, in the former textile/Sprague Electric Co. mills.

At No. Adams' Heritage State Park, various interactive displays about tunnel building and railroading are featured.

CROSS COUNTRY

HISTORIC VALLEY CAMPGROUND

1.5 or 2.0 mi. loops. Elevation: 960 ft. Novice.

Road approaches

Follow E. on Main St. to Church St. Turn right, pass No. Adams State College, and then left on Bradley St., which more or less ends at Windsor Lake, a town-owned recreation area. (A planned housing development straight ahead may alter the road pattern.) Turn right to the Windsor Lake parking lot. At the beach area the city of No. Adams erects a map of the ski trails in the winter.

HISTORIC VALLEY CAMPGROUND

Follow along the lake shore, through a fence that marks Historic Valley itself (a city-run camping area in the summer). Bear right past the corner of the recreation building and above the trailers. Follow "xc ski" signs on a level stretch through the woods, past camping sites. A cutoff for the shorter loop enters right. Follow along the trail for the longer loop, also eventually turning right.

Other trails wander through the area, much of which is former fields turned into second growth. If you continue straight instead of turning right, you eventually wind down to a stream; turning right again takes you on a heavily snowmobiled woods road to the western portal of the Hoosac railroad tunnel. This excursion has considerably more up and down than the campground loops.

The longer of these takes you over a narrow bridge. The cutoff enters right. You continue back to the parking lot. The open stretch near the lake gives a fine panorama of the hills and valleys of No. Adams.

FLORIDA AND SAVOY

In 1753 Capt. Elisha Hawley, commander at Fort Massachusetts, then the westernmost wilderness outpost of the Bay Colony and now No. Adams, began to build the first road east over the mountains to Charlemont, largely following an Indian route, to provision his fort. The road climbed to the Western Summit (as it's called now) about as does present Rte. 2 but then followed the line of what is now Central Shaft Rd. to the Cold River, west of the present highway. Samuel Rice, a few years later, built a route closer to the present one, up from Charlemont; for some reason he generally gets all the credit. But then, the Trail is in the Mahican Indian hunting grounds, yet the auto road is called the Mohawk Trail. The first Savoy settlers, in 1777, called the wet, rocky town, located at nearly 2,000 ft. in elevation, New Seconk, but at its incorporation it was named after the mountainous Savoy section of Europe. Florida was incorporated in 1805, at a time when the whole country was excited about a proposed land purchase from Spain. New State Rd., by the way, was not named for a construction project by the Commonwealth, but a religious community active in the area in the 19th century.

In those days Savoy and Florida were busy farming and manufacturing towns. You come across many cellar holes, mill sites, and cemeteries, as well as old roads. The lack of good farm land and the appeal to go west, especially after the opening of the Erie Canal in 1825, drained this hilly land of its population. On February 9, 1875, the first three flatcar-loads of dignitaries passed beneath Florida, signaling the opening of the Hoosac Tunnel, then the longest in the world (4.75 mi.); more convenient than Hawley's provisioning route. The state purchased a few acres around Borden Mtn. in order to erect a fire tower there in 1917, adding 10,000 acres in 1920 to fill out Savoy Mtn. State Forest. Construction of the Mohawk Trail led the state to purchase 3,000 acres for the Mohawk Trail State Forest in 1921, the first state camp grounds. Over the years, the state has added more land in Florida and Savoy to its holdings, so that it now owns fully half of Savoy.

Several CCC units made camp in Savoy in the 1930s. They built many of the dams and the roads, together with stone culverts and bridges. They also planted vast areas of spruce in order to provide for a forestry industry. They built the cabins at South Pond and the picnic facilities at North Pond. Forest HQ is located in former CCC buildings. There was a camp at the parking lot at Burnett and New State roads. and one at Tannery Falls. The CCC "boys" must have cursed the blackflies in the summer and the snow, which accumulates deeper here than anywhere else in the county, in the winter. In fact, one vicious winter storm nearly flattened one of their bunkrooms.

Camping

The Savoy Mtn. State Forest camping area is located on South Pond, a mile south of forest HQ on Central Shaft Rd. As well as tent and trailer sites (no hookups but toilets and showers), 3 very popular cabins, used year around, look out over the pond. No reservations are accepted for any state campsites, but the cabins must be reserved in advance (413-663-8469). The state maintains a campground a few miles east on Rte. 2, at Mohawk Trail State Forest. Chilson's Pond Campground, north of Rte. 2 at Whitcomb's Summit, is privately owned.

Road approaches

From Dunkin' Donuts on Rte. 2 in No. Adams, follow E. on Rte. 2, up around the Hairpin Turn and farther up into Florida. After you pass the Wigwam Gift Shop, bear right at the second turning (5.0 mi.), where a chocolate and white sign directs you to Savoy Mtn. State Forest. Bear right at the next 2 intersections. Both are signed. On your left is the ventilation shaft, originally a construction shaft, for the Hoosac railroad tunnel, 583 ft. below. Hence the name of the road: Central Shaft. Pass forest HQ on the right. Next on the right is the trailhead for the Spruce Hill hike where Old Florida Rd. enters. Your starting point is the North Pond parking lot, which soon appears on the right.

CROSS COUNTRY

NORTH POND LOOP

3.1 mi. Elevation: 1,900 to 2,200 ft. Intermediate.

This loop is best toured clockwise, so that the steepest part on the narrowest trail is up and much of the down is on a wide woods road. Not overly challenging, it's an enjoyable short run, which you may like so much you decide to do it twice. Everywhere along this route are opportunities for elaborating on the basic loop, including skiing the frozen surfaces of North or South ponds. At the pond the elevation is 1,900 ft.; the height of the ridge rises to 2,200 ft. The best view is N. of North Pond, over Tower Swamp to Spruce Hill.

As well as the possibility of camping overnight in a cabin at South Pond, you might want to consider bringing charcoal and starter fluid, and something to cook on the grills at North Pond. At first the idea of standing in the snow to cook out may seem strange, but it grows on you. Water is available if you cut through the ice in the pond, or you can bring a beverage. Do not leave any trash, however.

A sign by the parking area has maps of the trails. Ski toward the pond and left on the service road. Just before the gate at Central Shaft Rd., jog right, into the woods. Continue to turn right at each subsequent trail junction. In effect you will follow S., climb over the ridge you saw across the pond, ski along its far side, and return around the end of the ridge, near Central Shaft Rd. again.

Turn right where a trail enters (left) from the road, among sizable hemlocks. Climb a small rise to the next trail junction, where trails enter from South Pond. Start climbing, steeply, up the side of the ridge, including bearing left at a junction. The trail forms a large S as it rises to the summit and follows S. along the ridge.

At a sharp turn it starts down until it comes out on a woods road. Stay right, following this road over several brook crossings (you may have to take off your skis to cross) until yet another trail enters left. Both of the last 2 head for Old Florida Rd., formerly open between Adams and Florida via Central Shaft Rd.

A fine view N. opens over the swamp, revealing Spruce Hill, a summit you can ski to, and smaller peaks. As the woods road nears Central Shaft Rd. it turns right and winds down to the service road. Ski around or under the gate to return to the beginning.

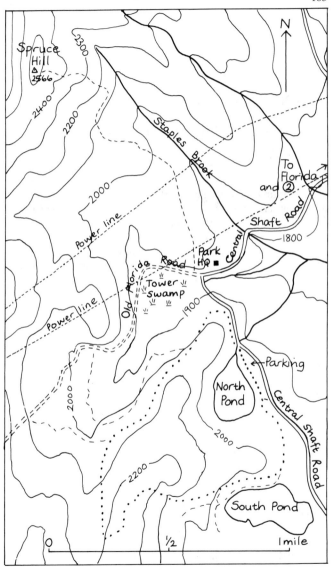

FLORIDA AND SAVOY: NORTH POND LOOP

OUTSIDE THE COUNTY

Although Berkshire County offers virtually limitless opportunities for skiing, variety is said to spice life. Within a half hour or so of the county lie challenging downhill and premiere cross country sites. Furthermore, those in the highlands just to the E. and just to the N. serve to lengthen the nordic season, holding snow when grass is showing in Berkshire. The southern Vermont snowbelt averages 100 inches of snow a winter, one-third more than North County. Berkshire County high school and college nordic teams head for some of these hills when conditions aren't satisfactory on the home courses. You should know about them, too.

PETERSBURG, New York

CROSS COUNTRY

SNOW HOLE

5.0 mi. Elevation: 2,090 to 2,400 ft. Novice.

Road approaches

From Field Park in Williamstown drive S. on Rtes. 7 & 2 to south Williamstown. Follow Rte. 2 (the Taconic Trail) W., rising 4 mi., from 850 ft. where the roads divide to 2,090 ft. at the pass. You are now in Petersburg, New York. Needless to say, the snow cover and general weather will alter considerably over this rise. Take an extra layer of clothing. Park in the lot on the S. at the pass.

SNOW HOLE

A good way to get a fine, relatively level ski in at above 2,000 ft. is to let your car gain the elevation for you. The ski along the Taconic Crest Trail (TCT) N. of Petersburg Pass offers some good views to the S. and W., and some high exhilaration. The skiing itself, with a couple of brief exceptions, is easy, although you do have to scramble up the side of the pass at the beginning. The distance may be too much for complete beginners, however.

The New York State Forest Preserve exists because of the efforts of a former Williams College faculty member and New York State Department of Environmental Conservation Commissioner, Thomas Jorling. (Be careful getting in and out of the lot, due to traffic coming around the corner from the W.) You must cross the road and climb a sharp hill on the other side — you see the route others have used — until the slope reduces enough that you feel comfortable in putting on your skis. A premier view is this first, open slope area, back to Berlin Mtn. and W. into the valley of the Little Hoosic River.

Soon after entering the woods you descend, cross a spring, and rise. This is the most difficult section to negotiate on the entire trail. The Shepard's Well Trail exits right at the yellow sign (see the RRR Brooks Trail description), but you continue following the white, triangular blazes. To be sure, white blazes don't always show up in the winter; nevertheless, this trail is obvious except in a few spots where summer vehicular traffic, now forbidden, has created mudholes and then detours around them.

You follow along to the N. of a fine, open hill, known as Smith Hill. If time and conditions allow, you might like to take a brief sidetrip to the summit for the excellent view in all directions. Back on the TCT, continue N. in the trees along the ridge. The Birch Brook Trail enters left. You drop down into an opening and rise up the other side, leaving a private trail to your right. Soon you ski out of New York State into a corner of Vermont. The boundaries are cut but otherwise unidentified. You're now at about 2,300 ft.

You ski through 4 overlooks, of which the third is the best. Depending on sky conditions, you may see the Catskills and Albany. All face W., down into Petersburg, New York, and beyond, although they also reveal where you've come from. It's unlikely that the fourth would be a good picnic site in the winter, because of the wind that blows over the Taconic ridge, but it is a good place to turn around, reversing course back toward your start. Before returning, however, you may want to go a little farther to take a look into the Snow Hole which is protected by woods. To get there, go about .5 mi. beyond the turnaround point, to where the trail starts descending. The actual Snow Hole is a few hundred ft. in on a trail to the right of the TCT. It provides a good name for this route, but a snow hole — a deep crevasse where snow lingers long into the summer — is somewhat redundant when you're skiing.

The Snow Hole is an exposed part of a crack that seems to run a mi. or more to the E. (Vermont) side of the trail, most of it covered by thick foliage. But, again, summer seems more suitable for this kind of geological research. Your trip back, through the beech forest, should be similar to that coming in, except that the views will be even better. Exercise care when you sense you are nearing the verge of Rte. 2, where the trail drops with accelerating steepness. You probably want to take off your skis on the way back sooner than you put them on on the way up. Be careful crossing Rte. 2.

189

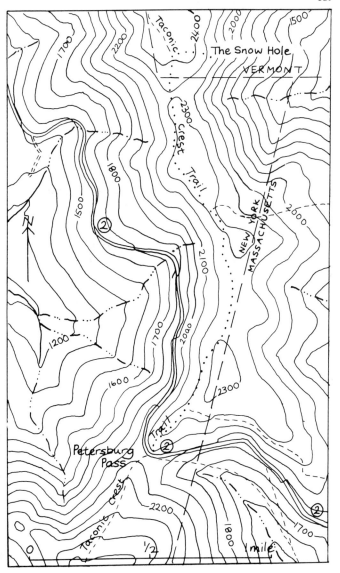

PETERSBURG, New York: SNOW HOLE

WORTHINGTON, Hampshire County

CROSS COUNTRY

HICKORY HILL

To arrive at these lovely wooded trails in Worthington, from most of Berkshire County, follow Rte. 8 to Rte. 143 E. from Hinsdale and through Peru. Hickory Hill is a mi. from its sign at the junction of Rtes. 143 and 112 in the center of Worthington. The elevation of about 1,600 ft. at the touring center stretches the season, as does the immaculate grooming that the owners, Catherine Rude and Timothy and Paul Sena apply to the trails.

Snaking out from the Big Field, are 25 km. of trails on 650 acres of rolling country, rising to 1,850 ft. The large barn features a fireplace and snack bar. Victuals include home-baked goods and soup-of-the-day, wine and malt beverages. Lessons, rentals, reduced rates for children, half-day rates and seasonal memberships. **238-5813.**

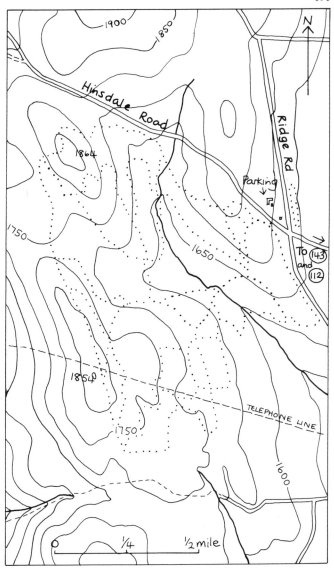

WORTHINGTON, Hampshire Co.: HICKORY HILL

CHARLEMONT, Franklin County

DOWNHILL

BERKSHIRE EAST

Trails: 25 (7 Novice; 9 Intermediate; 9 Expert). Summit elevation: 1,720 ft. Vertical drop: 1,180 ft. Lifts: 4 double chairs, 1 J-Bar, 1 T-Bar. 75% snowmaking. Ski School, Ski Shop, Rentals, 2 Cafeterias, Night skiing on 3 slopes and 2 trails. Snowboarding not allowed. On South River Rd., Charlemont, just off Rte. 2 (visible as you approach from the W.). **339-6617.**

Appropriately named for its location—a mountain pocket on the eastern side of the Hoosac Range — Berkshire East is on the edge of the Berkshires. Although its summit elevation is a few hundred ft. lower than most Berkshire areas, its 1,189 vertical drop puts it in the same league as the higher Catamount, Butternut, Brodie Mtn. and Jiminy Peak resorts. At least 2 trails, the Lift Line and Flying Cloud, validate its boast of being "Southern New England's most challenging ski area." Both plunge, straight as arrows, for 4,200 ft. beneath or alongside the 2 summit chairlifts.

Intermediate alternatives from the summit are Big Chief and Chute, with Chute steep at the top then leveling off and widening for a straight-down-the-mountain trail. Big Chief is a more winding route with steep pitches followed by runouts. Another favorite, for better skiers, is the Minnie Dole.

There's also a nice, easy trail from the top, the 2-mi. Mohawk that first heads E. and then does an about-face, affording views in both directions. Berkshire East also offers some delightful beginner terrain, consisting of a wide-open slope in front of the main lodge and 2 separate open slope areas just to the W. of the main lodge. Beginners have the areas on the western side all to themselves.

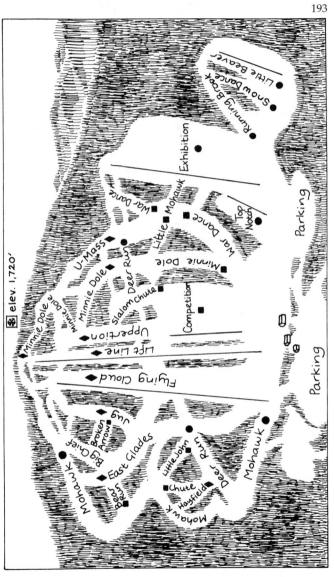

CHARLEMONT, Franklin Co.: BERKSHIRE EAST

The view from the summit is spectacular. The mountain is like a wall bordering the fairly narrow Deerfield River valley, and from the top skiers can literally peer straight down, almost as if they were in a balloon. Looking W., the Deerfield Valley narrows with mountains crowding the river, finally disappearing at the point where the Mohawk Trail (Rte. 2) begins to thread its way over the mountains to Berkshire County (Florida and No. Adams) on the other side.

The main lodge is rustic and offers an upstairs bar. A second lodge on the W. end is conveniently located near the beginners' slope, and like the main lodge, features a full cafeteria.

Visitors won't find a great many people from the Berkshires at Berkshire East, even though it attracts a hardcore following from the county. That's because its location isolates it from the county's main traffic patterns. They will, however, see lots of skiers from the Connecticut River valley: Springfield, Holyoke, Amherst, Northampton and Greenfield. They are the bread-and-butter customers and many of them ski nights when 5 main trails and slopes are open, including Flying Cloud and Big Chief from the top. Berkshire East is definitely a sleeper as far as Berkshire County is concerned, and offers a variety of enjoyable downhill skiing terrain.

HAWLEY, Franklin County

CROSS COUNTRY

STUMP SPROUTS

This ski touring center, one of the most spectacular scenic layouts around, looks down into the deep gorge of Chickley River, a tributary of the Deerfield. The philosophy is to maintain narrow, winding trails, to retain intimacy for the skier and low impact on the environment, while still providing for grooming. The management is developing some skating trails, however.

West Hill Rd. is 6.6 mi. S. of Rte. 2 (the Mohawk Trail) on Rte. 8-A from Charlemont. Thus Stump Sprouts makes a good companion to Berkshire East, the downhill area. West Hill Rd., running W. of 8-A, while surfaced, is extremely steep. The ski center, at an old farmhouse, provides a warming area, rentals and lessons. There are accommodations at the lodge, behind the barn. Those who wish to use these trails on weekdays should call ahead. **339-4265.**

The grand variety of trails, more rigorous than those of most touring centers, climb from 1,500 ft. at the farmhouse to 1,870 ft. at Lone Boulder Hill, where there is a 3-state lookout (Massachusetts, Vermont, New Hampshire). Primitive sections of trails are not groomed. Still, many km. of trails are in the easiest category, including skiing on unplowed roads.

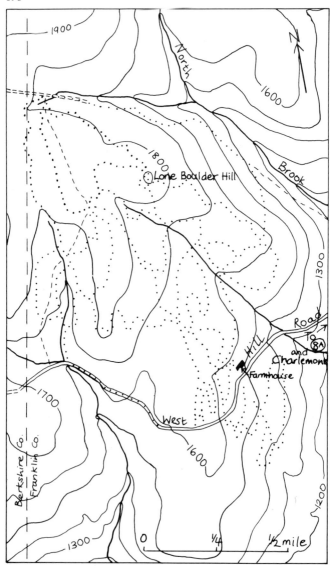

HAWLEY, Franklin Co.: STUMP SPROUTS

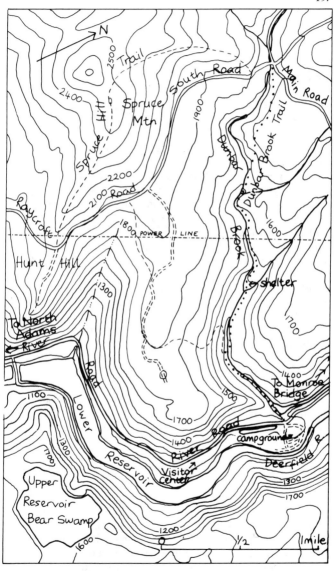

MONROE, Franklin Co.: DUNBAR BROOK

MONROE, Franklin County

CROSS COUNTRY

DUNBAR BROOK

Four sites have been set aside in western Massachusetts as "Backcountry Areas," undeveloped and remote state-owned land. In addition to Dunbar Brook, the others are the Cold River old-growth forest, the Hopper on Mt. Greylock and Alander Mtn. In and out, the Dunbar Brook tour length described here is 2.5 hrs. Skiing along this brook under heavy hemlock cover is a special experience — worth driving down and back up the steep road, problematic in winter, that takes you from Rte. 2 (the Mohawk Trail) in Florida down to the village of Hoosac Tunnel.

Drive to the top of the Mohawk Trail, E. from No. Adams on Rte. 2. After Whitcomb Summit, take the next left, then the next right. You head steeply down to a T at River Rd. The river is the Deerfield. Go left at the T, through the village of Hoosac Tunnel, across the tracks exiting from the eastern portal of the tunnel, and right by Bear Swamp Visitors Center. You want to park on the left, .75 mi. N. of the Visitors Center, 4.5 mi. from the Mohawk Trail, — but that area may not be plowed. If not, pull into the road, right, that leads to a campground.

The state and New England Power Company jointly maintain the trail, across Monroe State Forest land. Start up the hill, left, then follow the blue blazes into the woods. The trail, narrow here, falls and rises and falls, crossing two small bridges. Do not be put off. This is the most difficult portion. After a mi. you cross a major bridge, resting on telephone poles, over Dunbar Brook. The rest of the trail is wide, rising gently on the N. side of the waterway. At .5 mi. beyond the bridge, after a side brook crossing for which you may have to remove your skis, you pass a three-sided shelter. Just beyond are some interesting foundations. A good lunch spot, this could be your destination, although you would miss the most awe-inspiring section of hemlock forest still to come. You cross under powerlines and then, after another .5 mi., the trail swings sharply uphill, past a large boulder. You might wish to stop in the lovely, wide-open hemlock glen at that turn, as the next stretch of trail is not a safe ski on the return unless the snow is deep. If you do continue on, in .25 mi. you will reach the South Rd. bridge over Dunbar Brook, at the junction of South and Main Rds. (in Monroe, Franklin County).

Main Rd., which becomes Tilda Hill Rd. and joins the Mohawk Trail in Florida, is plowed, so a car could meet you there; although on a 2-car trip you would probably want to ski the other direction, downstream. If your car won't make it up Whitcomb Hill Rd. on the return, go down River Rd. at the T, across the Deerfield, and through Zoar to Rte. 2.

STAMFORD, Vermont

CROSS COUNTRY

YAW POND

The 4.5 mi. round-trip ski into Yaw Pond is a special introduction to the hundreds of miles of trails and woods roads, all skiable, in southern Vermont. Here is backcountry skiing as you always hoped it would be. For an overview, you may want to order the "1988 Vermont Recreation Plan" from the Agency of Natural Resources, 103 South Main St., Waterbury, VT 05676.

Drive Rte. 8, N. from No. Adams, through Clarksburg, MA and Stamford, VT (Rte. 8 becomes Rte. 100 in Vermont). Follow uphill past the former Dutch Hill Ski Area and .5 mi. down the other side to the bottom of the hill. There, a new section of road cuts off a sharp corner at the bridge at 1,808 ft. in elevation, in case you have an altimeter in your car. The Old Stage Rd. enters, following along the West Branch of the Deerfield River. This road, not normally plowed, may be for logging, but it is possible to ski along the left. It is the start of your adventure.

Signs welcome winter sports types to Green Mtn. National Forest. Even without lumber trucks, snowmobiles are extremely busy on this section, but after 1.1 mi. you will turn on to a lesser-used trail. You rise on this woods road and then drop downhill to a bridge. A trail on the left, by the brook, may be open for most of this stretch. Do not cross the bridge; rather, turn right along Yaw Pond Brook. Swing right again almost immediately, rather than crossing the old footbridge. The trail is marked with triangular, green blazes. You are now in a hemlock forest, following beside the brook, gently uphill for .8 mi.

Remarkably, you come to a signed intersection, in the middle of the woods. Do not go right to Wilmington and the Motel-on-the-Mountain." Bear left, over the bridge, to "Woodford and Bennington." You come out in .2 mi. on

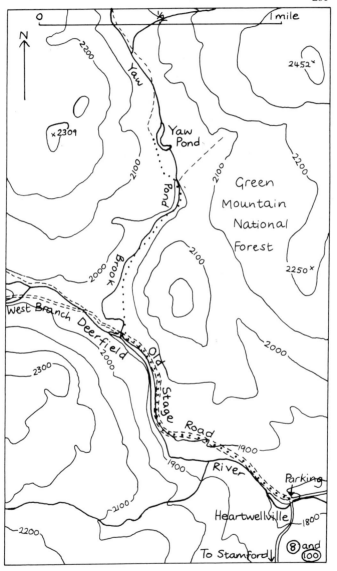

STAMFORD, Vermont: YAW POND

the beaver-infested Yaw Pond. The winter trail runs across it; the foot trail passes to the W. The Pond, at 2,000 ft., is a fine destination and, on a sunny day, a good spot for lunch. Here's the warning label, however: the going is so nice you may want to continue N., even if you'd planned to go no farther. If you do continue N., eventually you cross another heavily traveled snowmobile way; 3.0 mi. from the pond, along the Kelly Camp Trail, and you come out on Rte. 9 in Woodford, VT at 2,200 ft. — .5 mi. E. of the next ski site (Prospect Mtn.).

BENNINGTON, Vermont

DOWNHILL/CROSS COUNTRY

PROSPECT MOUNTAIN

Downhill Trails: 7, Novice to Intermediate. Summit elevation: 2,876 ft. Vertical drop: 726 ft. Lifts: 2 T-Bars, 1 rope tow. XC Trails: 13. Ski School, Ski Shop, Rentals, Cafeteria. Open daily for xc; downhill: wkends and holiday wks. only. On Rte. 9, 8 mi. E. of Bennington, VT. **802-242-2575**

Prospect Mtn., a pocket-size alpine and cross country ski area, is one of the few areas in New England without snowmaking. But with elevations of 2,150 at the base and 2,876 at the summit, along with a clientele that is 75 percent cross country skiers, Prospect doesn't need to make snow the way the others do. For a shortcut to Prospect from the Berkshires and S., which is also a beautiful drive, leave Rte. 7 on Barber Pond Rd., up the hill from Pownal. Stay on the paved road around the pond and N. on W. Branch Brook Rd. until you come out on Rte. 9. Turn right.

Prospect appeals to families with hotshot cross country skiers, particularly skaters, and alpine skiers who are either beginners or intermediates. The area is also popular for telemarking, a style of skiing that blends alpine and cross country techniques into a free heel downhill turn. The trail next to the longer T-Bar lift is the toughest on the mountain. All of the others are wide, with gentle pitches and sweeping views of the southern Vermont mountainscape. Because the area is small, friends are made easily with distinctions between staff, guests and volunteer helpers blurred. This is particularly true in the cafeteria where conversation flows easily from table to table.

The cross country trail layout at the base offers 40 km. of groomed trails with one of them a gradual climb up the back side of the mountain to the summit and then providing access to other trails, many of them logging roads, in Woodford State Park.

In bad winters (meaning too little snow), Prospect is usually the best bet close to Berkshire County for xc skiing, offering a season that begins early and ends late. The alpine trails are best suited for families with young skiers and telemarkers. A climb to the summit on the Mountain Trail, using telemark skis and climbing skins, followed by a telemark trip down the alpine trails can be most enjoyable.

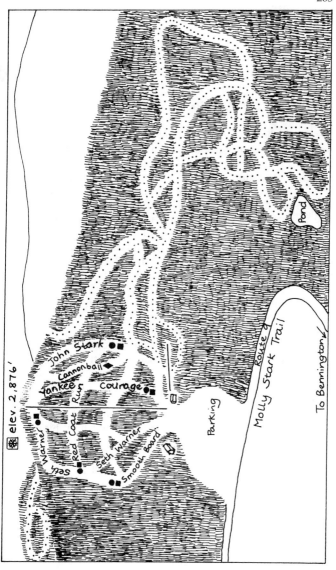

BENNINGTON, Vermont: PROSPECT MOUNTAIN

WOODFORD, Vermont

CROSS COUNTRY

WOODFORD STATE PARK

For the heaviest snow cover south of. . . Stowe, probably, welcome to Woodford State Park. Look to the right 3.0 mi. beyond Prospect Mtn. Ski Area, also on the right, on Rte. 9 out of Bennington. Of course skiing is good here any time of the winter, at 2,200 ft. in the southern Vermont snowbelt, but it is most famous locally as a place to stretch the season. The service roads for the state camping area, located on Adams Reservoir, are unplowed and available for skiers — snowmobilers, too, but more exotic trails call most of them. Rather than parking along the soft shoulder of Rte. 9 (with traffic whizzing by at 55 m.p.h.), park 100 yards E. and across the road at a designated spot.

The state does not want you to ski the hiking trail, which circumnavigates the pond, until it has had a chance to make some improvements in it. You enter by a swamp, pass the summer camp buildings, then have a choice of bearing right, ending anticlimactically in a gravel pit; following a trail straight, which opens on to the reservoir; or swinging left, down below the earth dam. This is the most fruitful choice in terms of alternatives, which begin to branch off as you climb the hill beyond the bridge. The grid of roads tours the campgrounds; the around-the-pond trail, blazed blue, with steep drops, bears off left. Although not groomed, sufficient numbers of snowmobiles use the roads to provide good snow packing for skating as well as diagonal xc skiing.

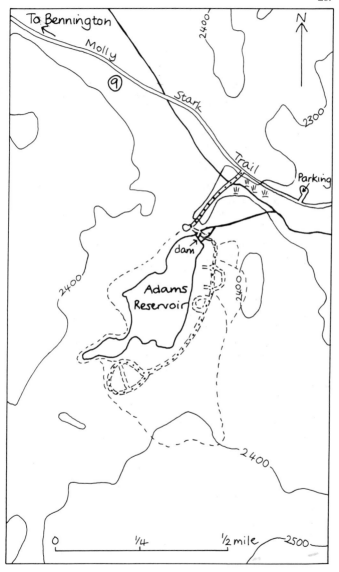

To Bennington

Molly

9

Stark

Trail

Parking

2400

2300

dam

2400

Adams
Reservoir

2400

2400

2400

2500

0   ¼   ½ mile

WOODFORD, Vermont: WOODFORD STATE PARK

APPENDICES

XC SKI TRAILS BY DEGREE OF DIFFICULTY

Many of the cross country areas, including all the commercial ski centers, mentioned in this book present the skier with a range of trails from easy to difficult. Standard national symbols are used in most developed areas. A green disk with a white, wavy line across it represents trails designed for beginners over gently sloped terrain. A blue square with a steeper white wavy line is suited for intermediates. You should be able to stop on the steeper terrain with a good snowplow. The black diamond with a white zigzag denotes trails reserved for experts who can turn and stop effectively in close quarters. Many areas also put up caution signs that may mean a trail crosses at the bottom of a hill, a sharp turn or something else unexpected. The area managers assign the ratings, so there is some variation in standards.

A rating follows for the tours specifically described here, using the same scale: Novice, Intermediate, Expert, in the order they are presented in this book.

SOUTH COUNTY

Ashley Hill I
Mt. Everett I
Bartholomew's Cobble ....N
Abbey Lake ....N
Simon's Rock ....N
Butternut I
Beartown State Forest ....N,I,E
Oak N' Spruce ....N
Tyringham Cobble I
Bowker's Woods ....N

CENTRAL COUNTY

Canterbury Farm .... N,I,E
Bucksteep Manor .... N,I,E
October Mtn. .... N
Kennedy Park .... N,I
Pleasant Valley .... N
Berry Pond I
Canoe Meadows .... N
Kirvin Memorial Park .... N
Shaker Mountain I
Rice Sanctuary .... N,I
Notchview Reservation .... N,I

NORTH COUNTY

Hoosic River Railroad .... N
Brodie Ski Touring Center .... N,I,E
Rockwell Rd. I
Bellows Pipe .... E
Cheshire Harbor .... E
Roaring Brook/Stony Ledge .... E
Stone Hill I
RRR Brooks .... E
Hopkins Forest .... N,I,E
Field Farm .... N
Mt. Greylock Ski Club .... N,I
Historic Valley Campground .... N
North Pond Loop I

OUTSIDE THE COUNTY

Snow Hole .... N
Hickory Hill .... N,I,E
Stump Sprouts .... N,I,E
Dunbar Brook I
Yaw Pond .... N
Prospect Mtn. .... N,I,E
Woodford State Park I

OTHER WINTER SPORTS

Some winter sport depends on wintery weather. You can skate, for example, on 100 ponds and lakes, provided only that you are willing to shovel off the snow. On Pontoosuc Lake that duty is taken care of, especially around the time of the speed skating championships. Portions of smaller ponds are also cleared, but it is hard to predict when. Let opportunity be your guide. Although the ice on ponds can be rough and the wind or precipitation annoying, it is a special treat to skate outside among the mountains. Pittsfield Parks Department floods fields for skating, as do other public and private entities throughout the county. To find nearby areas, you can call your local town office to see when and where flooding will be done for ice skating.

Among the skating sites to check out, the Stockbridge Bowl has a double inducement. Not only can the ice be glass but access — at the boat ramp off Rte. 183 — is easy, compared to the summer when you must be a local resident or belong to the boat club to enjoy its splendors. Still, the Bowl is a bit big and subject to the biting wind. Laurel Lake in Lee, with easy access from Rte. 20, and Cheshire Reservoir, reached from the roadside rest at the N. end, are inviting.

Even more sheltered but harder to get to are Benedict Pond, on a gravel road off Rte. 23 in Beartown State Forest, and North Pond on Central Shaft Rd., off Rte. 2 in Florida-Savoy. You could pretty much have the ice to yourself. If you'd prefer town access, Card Lake, on Rtes. 41 or 102, is near the center of W. Stockbridge and the Mass. Turnpike exit. Eph Pond in Williamstown is just down the hill from the Williams College Field House, on the N. side of the campus. Usually students have cleared off the snow.

Most people, to be less romantic, find it easier to skate inside. The Chapman Rink at Williams College, 597-2283, Vietnam Veteran's Memorial Rink in No. Adams (the only place you can rent skates in the county), 664-9474, and the Pittsfield Boys Club, 448-8258, are all open to the public with reduced rates for children.

Lakes get other winter uses. Occasionally Pontoosuc is the scene of official ice automobile races. Fishermen get their largest catches through the ice, especially northern pike. Shacks appear on Pontoosuc, Onota, and Cheshire Reservoir, although you can often find the fishermen at work on the smaller ponds — which, incidentally, tend not to be as exposed to the wind. Fishermen must have a license at all times of the year.

Sleighing is not a thing of the past, although usually the "sleighs" are more like wagons with rubber-tired wheels now. Such hay rides are regularly a part of the Christmas Walk through the shopping streets of Williamstown a few weeks before Christmas. The Williams Inn, like other country inns, offers horse-drawn rides during the holidays. It takes you back: the harness bells, some caroling, bundling together to keep warm, the steam rising off the horses. . . The horses come out again at the end of winter to give rides around the sugar bush and maple sugaring time or at demonstrations of maple sugaring, as at Hancock Shaker Village.

Sledding, tobogganing, traying. . . the variety of wooden, plastic or cardboard aids to sliding down a hill is only limited by the imagination. The number of hills is in no way limited. Perhaps the most public places to slide in all of Berkshire County are the hills at Clapp Park on W. Housatonic St., and in front of the Reid Middle School on North St. in Pittsfield. The third most public would be in front of Monument Mt. Regional High School, on Rte. 7 between Gt. Barrington and Stockbridge. There, a grassy slope runs out on the soccer field. Golf courses get their share of sledders. In Williamstown, the best sledding on the Taconic course is on the Green River Rd. (Rte. 43) side. Many ski areas have a place set aside for children to sled, as at Prospect and the Mt. Greylock Ski Club. As well as sledding in open fields, the more adventuresome might like to try some of the unplowed roads. You could slide for miles on a toboggan in October Mtn. or Beartown state forests, for example, although you would have to look out for snowmobiles. And you would have to walk back up.

Some winter sports are actually ones associated with

other seasons that can also be played in the winter, such as tennis inside at Brodie Mtn. Tennis and Racquet Club, 499-3038; or the Racquet Club at Bousquet, 499-4600. Racquetball is also available at the YMCAs in Pittsfield, 499-7650; and No. Adams, 663-6529. The YMCA at Pittsfield has squash courts for public use. Williams College and private schools have them but they are not generally available. The two YMCAs have indoor pools, as does Williams College, 597-2366, and Berkshire Community College, 499-4660, as well as inns and resorts. Most have public rates. Some of the riding stables in the county have indoor riding rings.

SNOW AND SNOWMAKING

The Inuits of Kobuk Valley in Alaska have 16 words for different kinds of snow and snow formations, and no doubt profit from the exactness of their vocabulary. After all, their survival depends on recognizing and being able to deal with different snow conditions. The closest most New England skiers come to that precision may be the cross country skiing waxing chart, which prescribes different color wax for different temperatures and snow quality. That varies according to moisture: fine new snow, old powder snow, granular snow. Below freezing waxing is a snap: moderately cold, wax blue; very cold, wax green. At freezing and above things get complicated. Few skiers other than racers wax in these days of waxless skis.

Freezing rain arrives when temperatures are warm above and cold below, so that what falls as rain freezes when it hits the ground. Hailstones are raindrops that freeze on the way down. Sleet is a mixture of rain with snow or hail. Snow forms when water molecules, under frigid temperatures in the clouds, attach to each other in hexagonal patterns to form ice crystals. The crystals grow and join, in the air, to fall to the earth as flakes. As you already know, each snow flake is different.

When skiing began in this area in the 1930s, all snow was natural and everyone had to make his or her own way up to the top of the hill. Skiing was canceled if nature didn't cooperate. The more sophisticated tourist industry of today requires not only lifts but dependable snow cover, which nature will not provide. Little downhill skiing would have taken place in Berkshire on recent years without manipulating the snow cover. Now resort owners invest in fancy tractors to groom slopes, whether downhill or cross country, in order to maintain a loose surface on top and to cover any holes. Anyone who has descended one of the steeper Berkshire slopes in one of these vehicles will attest that skiing is not the only source of downhill thrills.

Berkshire ski resort owners observe: "If they can play

golf on Long Island, they don't think they can ski in Massachusetts." But they can, of course, ski in Berkshire even in warm weather, and advertising is designed to spread that message. In fact, they can ski in these hills while playing golf here, because of the resorts' big snow guns.

Snowmaking is an attempt under artificial conditions to reproduce what happens in the clouds. The basic approach is to create a water vapor by pumping compressed air and water through a nozzle or snow gun. The air helps break up the water droplets and propel them into the air. The density of snow that results depends on a variety of factors, including the temperature of the air and the humidity. As in nature, the colder the air and the lower the humidity, the drier the snow.

For downhill skiers, the best snow, according to John Lancaster, head of operations at Brodie Mtn., should be of "snowball packing quality." If it's too wet, skiers complain. If it's too dry, it blows away. Other factors that affect the quality of snow are the temperature of the water being pumped, the amount of water lost to evaporation and what those in the trade refer to as "hang time" — the amount of time the water is in the air before it hits the ground. The longer it hangs, the longer it has to freeze.

Snowmaking in recent years has been more efficient and more effective at temperatures nearing 32 degrees F. In nature a cubic foot of water will generally yield about 8 cubic ft. of snow. Manmade snow is much less productive, with a ratio of 1:2. To cover one acre with manmade snow to a depth of 2 ft. therefore takes 325,850 gallons which, even if the ski area has its own wells or a pond, it still has to pay to pump. Because of the large volume of water needed and because of the high energy costs of compressed air, ski resorts are continually looking for ways to increase the ratio of snow to water and reduce the use of compressed air.

Some companies, such as Hedco in New Jersey, produce "airless guns" or snow cannon. These guns inject tiny ice crystals as "nuceators" into low-pressure, high-volume air flow, from fans rather than compressed air. They are large, however, requiring several men and machines to move about. Snow cannons with their hoses and wires, on the slopes where people are skiing, can be a hazard, so areas seem to be turning more to permanently mounted guns on towers, their pipes and wires buried underground. The increased hang time adds efficiency, too.

The best way to work at higher temperatures is to introduce impurities into the water. The temperature of pure water has to be lowered to minus 40 degrees F. before it will form ice crystals and snow. Naturally occurring impurities, such as minerals, plant matter, microorganisms or organic chemicals will help flakes form at temperatures up to 14 degrees F. Since 1986, the Kodak Co. has been marketing Snomax snow inducer, naturally occurring bacteria with the scientific name Pseudomonas syringae that Kodak says will help form snow up to 28 degrees F.

Ski area operators calculate that it is worthwhile for them to pay the extra for Snomax if it means more hours of snowmaking on otherwise marginal days. An earlier opening for the season means extra income and a bonus in publicity. In Berkshire, there is high competition to open before Thanksgiving. But snowmaking doesn't stop when the real stuff begins to fall. Jiminy Peak, for example, budgets 1,000 to 1,200 hrs. of snowmaking per year. Brodie Mtn. cranks it out to a depth of 5 or 6 ft., to keep cover in case of a thaw. At what is known as Kelly's Irish Alps, Brodie wants to stay open at least to its annual St. Patrick's Day celebration, March 17, and preferably on into April. So it is not unusual, in these parts, to see snow guns operating at night while the real thing is fluttering down.

WHAT TO SEE IN WINTER

Even when the world becomes a study in muted shades, browns and whites like a daguerreotype, there remains much to see in the woods. According to Pamela B. Weatherbee, Williamstown naturalist, winter is a more subtle time of the year, although some natural signs are more pronounced than in the busy colors of spring, summer and fall.

On a 20-minute walk beside the Hoosic River, on a skiable trail cut by the Hoosic River Watershed Association, she pointed out a bouquet of animal and plant life continuing in the light snow cover. The trail across Williams College land runs W. from the Cole athletic fields off Cole Ave. to an access from Syndicate Rd., near North St. in Williamstown. The principles of observation could apply anywhere in Berkshire County, however.

Snow is a reverse blackboard that catches animals in their antics, their tracks the darker chalk marks, for many are active even in cold weather. Even if you don't see them, creatures run along or across the trail, which begins as a road and dwindles to woodsy path, with a detour to the gravel banks in the river bed. If it weren't for the snow, you would not know how active the animals were. It's easier to spot the tracks if you are among the first to venture that way since the last snowfall.

The white-footed mouse tracks, tiny paws grouped to jump, sometimes show a line left by the mouse's tail. Shrews and mice leave tunnels in the snow, revealed at a time of thaw, busy about their business of finding something green to gnaw on.

Weatherbee points out that all "cat tracks" are not made by cats. Cats, as opposed to dogs, walk Indian file with one foot directly in front of another, but so do other wild animals, so that the "big cat" tracks you saw may well have been made by a red fox. Bobcat can be found in remoter sections of the county, with wide paws functioning like snowshoes to hold them on top of the snow.

Squirrels and cottontail rabbits, too, have similar tracks, two smaller feet close together in front, with larger feet, wider apart, behind. Overall size of the tracks is not so much the difference as is the outsized rear rabbit feet. Deer leave the familiar, cloven-hoof marks, scattering their feet in clumps when they run, the way dogs do. The padded paw prints of dogs of all shapes and sizes are most familiar in most of our woods.

Down by the stream, muskrat and beaver move about in the winter, especially in the vicinity of any open water. The gold chips of gnawed trees left by beaver decorate the snow cover, often indicating the big furry fellow was at work quite recently — until your approach drove it away.

Sometimes signs in the snow tell stories: the mouse tracks move along until they disappear in a slight, snowy disturbance, suggesting an owl swooped down to make off with it. More of a disturbance, even some blood or fur, might suggest that an animal, perhaps a cat, caught a small creature.

Animal tracks

Many birds are active in the winter about these parts, although Weatherbee notes that you will be more apt to see chickadees and nuthatches at the feeder than in the woods. They have adapted well to human intervention.

Still, as well as traces of owl — being a night bird owls are not often seen — you can hear and see woodpeckers tapping on rotted tree trunks. Ducks still congregate in open water. Robins or cedar waxwings may be lurking in the glossy, red sumac berries.

The staghorn sumac berries do look something like an antler in velvet, clustered tightly together on a stalk. Weatherbee suggests soaking red sumac berries in water (do not heat — this isn't a tea) in order to make a drink that tastes something like lemonade.

The buttonballs on the sycamore (buttonwood) trees still cling to their branches. Down below, that swelling or gall on the dried goldenrod stem is the nursery for a wasp. The hole in the gall was probably pecked by a bird, looking to snack on infant wasp. The gall doesn't seem to injure the goldenrod, Weatherbee says.

The 3-ft.-or-more-tall canary grass along the riverways provides a tan background for a multitude of other plants with surprisingly different colors. Red-osier dogwood, for example, stands out from the crowd with its bright red branches. The red maple groves, as Henry David Thoreau said, look like grey smoke. The newest box elder branches are bluish, the weeping willows a golden color that seems to foretell spring all winter long.

If you would like to try your hand at dried floral arrangements, you might pick up some tansy, an herb, or wild rye grass, or dried aster, or Queen Ann's lace, with its flat top — all of which hold the shape of their summer flowers in winter along Berkshire trails.

Or you could look for some of the evergreen mosses, like club or Christmas fern, for which the deer scratch into the snow and leaves. Leave these splashes of green — do not dig up wild plants. Delicate wild cucumber vines decorate the deciduous trees, with their now tan-dry, pickle-shaped flowers.

The prickly multiflora roses, planted originally as living fences but escaped to the woods, add their substantial berry supply to the winter woodland scene. Down on the ground, you can see where the fiddles will form on the beaten down ostrich fern — when it greens up in early spring it will be ready for cooking.

Perhaps more subtle still, but instructive, winter allows you to recognize a tree by its shape rather than its leaf, a glimpse at the structure instead of the walls. The gross distinction between evergreens and deciduous is apparent, the pines, spruce, hemlock prominent as they seldom are in the summer.

Even those trees that have lost their leaves — the egg-shape formed by the sugar maple branches and the scraggly shape of the black willow; the squat, thick-branched oak, its silhouette wider than it is high, probably still retaining some of its leaves — reveal themselves, especially if they are growing relatively free from their fellows. Sycamore branches grow distinctively at a 90-degree angle from the mottled trunk, whereas on the beech, more delicate branches, starting almost

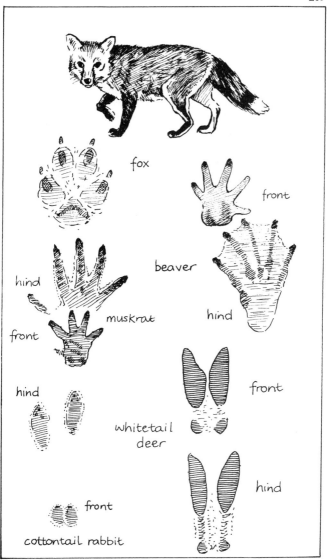

fox

front

beaver

hind

muskrat

hind

hind

front

whitetail
deer

front

hind

front

cottontail rabbit

at the base of the silvery trunk, reach skywards. The beech, too, retains some leaves late into the winter.

The birch bark is easily apparent, and decidedly different from the green of the aspen, although in leaf the two trees resemble each other. The white ash often divides its furrowed trunk down low. If you are lucky, you may see a young elm, its trunk narrowing like a bud vase and then spreading in a profusion of branches high up. Chances are the bark will be dropping off in strips, the tree done in by Dutch elm disease.

Plenty of things to look for in the winter; things to stop at and examine and speculate on; a winter ski need not be merely an assertion of the body's ability to function in snow and cold, but the mind's, as well. Wear warm clothes so that you can stay warm while you dawdle.

EQUIPMENT

Modern ski equipment is available in enough choices to produce anxiety about making the right pick. Don't worry. The great majority of equipment works well. Choices are much more a matter of individual preference than what's "right" or "wrong."

Even so, equipment for both cross country and or downhill skiing has become high tech. Alpine skis are fashioned from various exotic materials, boots are marvels of technology, and bindings have evolved into precision machines. As for cross country, ski offerings now come in wax, no-wax and skating styles, each one with a dozen variations. The same goes for telemark equipment. Each August, the ski magazines describe the latest equipment. It is impossible for any one store to carry a full inventory of what's available, yet magazines are a good place to start looking. While you don't have to be an expert on the equipment, you should be an expert on yourself. That means knowing how to describe accurately your own level of skiing and where you are likely to go. You should expect ski shop personnel to know the equipment they sell. You should expect salespeople to match the equipment to you. If you have doubts, go to another shop.

Perhaps the best way to find out about equipment is to rent it first, either from the ski store or from the ski area. Since on a busy weekend a ski area may have to outfit guests with skis that aren't quite right, ideally you should rent on weekdays. Many shops encourage renting and give rental customers a break on purchases of new equipment.

The cost of equipment varies widely during the season. Expect to pay premium prices between Thanksgiving and Christmas, but to discover real buys at the end of the season or during August and September pre-season sales. You can also save money by buying packages, which include skis, poles, bindings and boots.

Used Equipment

Huge savings can be achieved on purchases of both downhill and cross country equipment at used ski and skate sales, such as at the Pine Cobble School in Williamstown, at Jiminy Peak (to benefit the Hancock Fire Dept.), and at Kenver, the ski shop in So. Egremont. Such events make special sense for skiing families. Ski equipment is high tech and specific, however. The great advantage of buying new at a ski shop is the expertise of the shop personnel.

Downhill

The slalom ski, designed to make quick turns, is the most suitable for New England ski terrain, where trails are narrower and bumpier, the snow surface is packed harder, and there are more frequent patches of ice than in the west. The ski that floats through powder at Taos, New Mexico could be a disaster on Jiminy Peak's Exhibition trail. Although you may not notice the difference, the slalom ski has a narrower sidecut and is stiffer than a powder ski. "Sidecut" means that it is narrowest underneath the boot and widest at the shovel, just before the tip, a design that enables the ski to carve turns. More advanced skiers prefer the stiffer skis, because they can obtain more bite on turns and in tough spots. Beginner skiers, who want a ski to turn more easily, prefer softer skis that don't require such pronounced weighting and unweighting to bring them around.

While correctly chosen skis are important for performance, correctly fitted boots are critical for comfort. Modern boots are both warmer and lighter than their predecessors. Some leave nothing to chance, with battery-operated heaters. Novice skiers will want a softer boot that gives more flex for the effort; more advanced skiers will want stiffer boots. Whatever the ability level, however, the boot should cradle the foot firmly, leaving room to wiggle your toes. If the boot doesn't do this, keep trying other brands until one does. You will know when a boot fits right when heel, instep, toes and front of ankle feel supported but not pinched.

Buy as much in the bindings as you can afford and be sure they are compatible with your boots. You pay for the grade of steel and the precision of the mechanism. Cheap bindings are apt to lose their adjustment more quickly, either releasing too easily or not easily enough. Better bindings have a wide range of settings. They also give a little bit in a fall before releasing.

Poles are usually an afterthought. The better ones are stronger and lighter. Look for a pole with a grip that feels comfortable.

Downhill ski clothing should be warm, light and comfortable. Bib overalls as the basic garment are popular because they are form-fitting, keep the center of the body warm, and tuck in all other clothing. Ski clothing now is designed as a system that can be mixed and matched to meet the demands of weather and mood. Systems consist of outer shells, inner liners, bib overalls, overpants and vests. The garments are designed to be worn separately or to work together. Colors are bright. Fabrics repel rain and snow but allow ventilation.

Cross country

The technology of no-wax skis improves each year, so it is now possible to buy a ski that will work well in just about every condition. More proficient cross country skiers still point out that they don't get as much glide on no-wax skis in cold fresh snow conditions as on wax skis, but even diehards prefer them when the thermometer hits the freezing mark and snow varies between thaw and freeze.

Most cross country skiers should begin with a waxless ski bottom. If you plan to stay on trails with groomed tracks, use a lighter ski with less sidecut. Back-country skiers will want a heavier ski that is more responsive to turning initiatives. Mountaineers will want even heavier skis, preferably with steel edges.

The more camber your skis have — that is, the higher the arc under the boot section — the more will be demanded of your kicking technique. Beginners should have skis with soft camber that will send them along with mild kicks. Some skiers, especially younger ones, prefer the shorter skating ski over the more conventional diagonal stride ski. Skating is most enjoyable in areas with groomed trails, rather than in back country where snow varies and trails are narrow. Trails at touring centers often have set tracks at the sides, with the center groomed for skating. Skaters, by the way, wax for glide instead of kick.

Boots and bindings for cross country skiing are best bought as systems, which assure more stable connections, especially in snowplow turns. Boots range from lower and lighter to higher and heavier. Racers like the lighter boots for groomed surfaces. Skating boots are stiffer and higher than the diagonal stride variety. Higher boots are better for back country. Whatever you choose, the boot should feel soft and flexible around your foot, yet also firm enough to provide support. Make sure the boot doesn't bind the top of your toes, which could lead to painful blisters.

Pay more attention to selecting cross country poles than to alpine poles, because you use them for propulsion. Cheap poles break which makes it hard to ski cross country.

Equipment for telemark skiing—characterized by graceful turns that look like deep knee bends — falls between alpine and cross country. The steel-edge skis are heavier and wider than cross country skis but lighter and narrower than alpine skis. The same is true for telemark boots, which attach to 3-pin bindings as do many cross country ski boots.

Cross country ski clothing runs from loose-fitting old clothes, worn around the house in warmer seasons, to brightly colored high-tech body suits. Layers of lightweight clothing work best, because your work generates a lot of heat. Synthetic fabrics that wick moisture away from the body are popular. In spite of today's body suits, you still catch glimpses on the trail of men or women in wool hats, scarves, sweaters, knickers, and long stockings, once the only fashion of xc skiing.

Gaiters, waterproofed leggings that cover boot tops and fasten just below the knee, keep the snow out of your boots. Although unnecessary on groomed tracks, many skiers like their warmth and comfort.

Where to Rent or Buy Ski Equipment

All the downhill ski areas and some of the commercial cross country ski touring areas have ski shops that carry new and, sometimes, used equipment. The following Berkshire stores also sell ski equipment.

Arcadian Shop, Pittsfield-Lenox Rd. (Rte. 7), Lenox, 637-3010
Berkshire Outfitters, Rte. 8, Adams, 743-5900
Besse Clarke Ski Shop, 273 North St., Pittsfield, 499-1090
Goff's Sports Inc., Spring St., Williamstown, 458-3605
Kenver Ltd., Skip Shop, Rte. 23, So. Egremont, 528-2330
Klein's All-Sport Distributors, Berkshire Mall, Rte. 8, Lanesborough, 443-3531
Mountain Goat, 130 Water St., Williamstown, 458-8445
Outdoor Living, 585 S. Main St., Lanesborough, 445-4957
Plaine's Ski & Cycle Center, 55. W. Housatonic St., Pittsfield, 499-0391
Spoke Bicycles & Repair, 408 Main St., Williamstown, 458-3456
Sports, Inc., Allendale Shopping Ctr., Rtes. 8 and 9, Pittsfield, 442-1824
Tonon's Ski Haus, Rte. 7, Lanesborough, 443-0671

Bookstores

Many Berkshire area bookstores sell USGS topographical maps and other travel guides which you may find useful while visiting the region. See the Bibliography for suggestions.

Berkshire Bookshop (2 locations), 375 North St., Pittsfield; N. Adams Ctr., N. Adams
The Book Maze, Lenox House Country Shops, Rte. 7, Lenox
The Bookloft, Barrington Plaza, Rte. 7, Gt. Barrington
The Bookstore, 9 Housatonic St., Lenox
The College Book Store, Inc., Spring St., Williamstown
Either/Or Bookstore, 122 North St., Pittsfield
Lauriat's Books, Berkshire Mall, Rte. 8, Lanesborough
Railroad St. Books, 44 Railroad St., Gt. Barrington, MA
Village Bookstore, Park St., Adams
Waldenbooks, Berkshire Mall, Rte. 8, Lanesborough
Water Street Bookshop, 26 Water St., Williamstown

BIBLIOGRAPHY

Appalachian Trail Guide to Massachusetts-Connecticut (1988), Appalachian Trail Conference, P.O. Box 807, Harpers Ferry, WV, 25425-0807.

Binzen, William. *The Berkshires* (a book of photographs, 1986), Globe Pequot Press, Chester, CT.

Burns, Deborah, and Lauren R. Stevens. *Most Excellent Majesty: A History of Mount Greylock* (1988), Berkshire Natural Resources Council, 20 Bank Row, Pittsfield, MA 01201.

Caldwell, John. *The Cross-Country Ski Book* (1968), The Stephen Greene Press, Brattleboro, VT 05301.

Drew, Bernard. *A History of Notchview* (1987), Attic Revivals Press, Gt. Barrington, MA 01230.

Federal Writers Project. *The Berkshire Hills* (1939), reprinted (1987) by Northeastern University Press.

Griswold, Whit. *Berkshire Trails for Walking and Ski Touring* (1986), The East Woods Press (out-of-print).

Ryan, Christopher J. *Guide to the Taconic Trail System* (1989), New England Cartographics, P.O. Box 369, Amherst, MA 01004.

Sternfield, Jonathan. *The Berkshire Book: A Complete Guide* (1991), Berkshire House, P.O. Box 915, Gt. Barrington, MA 01230.

Stevens, Lauren R. *Hikes and Walks in the Berkshire Hills* (1990), Berkshire House, P.O. Box 915, Gt. Barrington, MA 01230.

Taconic Hiking Club. *Guide to the Taconic Crest Trail* (1989), 810 Church St., Troy, NY 12180.

Thoreau, Henry David. *A Week on the Concord and Merrimack Rivers* (1867), Ticknor and Fields. (1893) Houghton Mifflin Co., Boston, MA.

Williams Outing Club. *Trail Guide and Map* (1989), Williams College, Williamstown, MA 01267.

A Note on the Authors

Lauren R. Stevens, author with Deborah Burns of *Most Excellent Majesty: A History of Mount Greylock*, has lived and skied in Berkshire County for 27 of his 52 years. Founder in 1981 of *The Williamstown Advocate*, more recently, he has written on outdoor recreation and the environment for most Berkshire regional publications. He has also published a novel, *The Double Axe*, (Scribners). As an environmental consultant, he was principal author of *2003: A Study of Willamstown Over the Next 20 Years; The Hoosic River Action Plan;* and the GOALS study: *The Mount Greylock State Reservation.* The father of three, Lauren Stevens lives in Willamstown, where he has taught and served as Dean of Freshmen at Williams College. His *Hikes & Walks in the Berkshire Hills* was published by Berkshire House in 1990.

Lewis C. Cuyler, of Pittsfield, is also a longtime Berkshire resident and sportsman. His *Bike Rides in the Berkshire Hills* will be published in spring 1991 by Berkshire House. Lewis Cuyler is the editor of the business section of *The Berkshire Eagle.*